GOOD PRACTICE
IN THE EARLY YEARS

Related titles:
Janet Kay: *Protecting Children* (2nd edition)
Janet Kay: *A Teacher's Guide to Protecting Children*
Janet Kay: *Teaching Assistant's Handbook*
Carole Sharman, Wendy Cross and Diana Vennis: *Observing Children* (3rd edition)
John Triseliotis, Joan Shireman and Marion Hundleby: *Adoption: Theory, Policy and Practice* (2nd edition)

Good Practice in the Early Years

SECOND EDITION

Janet Kay

continuum
LONDON • NEW YORK

Continuum

The Tower Building   15 East 26th Street
11 York Road   New York
London SE1 7NX   NY 10010

First edition published as *Good Practice in Childcare* (2001).
Second edition published 2004. Reprinted 2005

British Library Cataloguing-in-Publication Data
A catalogue record for this book is available from the British Library.

ISBN   0–8264-7273-7 (paperback)

Designed and typeset by Ben Cracknell Studios
Printed and bound in Great Britain by Antony Rowe Ltd, Chippenham, Wiltshire

Contents

Preface

This book is intended to provide a basic understanding of good practice in early years care and education. It is aimed at a range of early years workers including nursery nurses, childminders, playgroup and pre-school workers, out-of-school care workers, classroom assistants and foster carers.

The book is structured to allow opportunities for self-assessment through a range of exercises in each chapter which can be used to reflect on what has been learned or to research an aspect further. The exercises are found in sections titled 'A Chance to Think'. Some of the exercises have sample answers for the relevant chapters in the Appendix. The sample answers are not meant to be the 'right' answers. Many of the exercises explore opinion, thoughts and feelings, so there are no 'right' answers. The sample answers are provided for you to check on the type of answer which may be appropriate and to compare your own views with another's. Some of the exercises relate to case studies which are used to explore work practice with children in different settings.

In order to keep the text simple the term 'parent' has been used to describe any person who acts as a parent to a child. This could include foster carers, grandparents, step-parents or anyone else who normally lives with and takes care of the child on a day-to-day basis and has primary responsibility for the child's welfare. The term 'early years worker' or 'early years practitioner' is used to describe anyone who has the care of children other than their own, in either a voluntary or paid capacity, whether this is in their own home or outside the home in a nursery, playgroup, school or crèche, for example.

For further simplicity the practice of referring to a child as 'she or he' or 's/he' has been avoided. Instead, the child has been referred to as either 'she' or 'he' on a random basis throughout the book. The term 'child' is generally used to refer to children up to 8 years old, as the book is aimed mainly at early years practitioners. However, in many areas the contents are applicable to children of a wider age range and the issues and questions raised by the case studies and exercises could be applied to a variety of settings and age groups.

The term 'early years care and education' is used to describe the role of early years workers with children. In recent years, the distinctions between education and care have been eroded and it is generally believed that the two are inextricably linked. As such, all early years workers care for and also educate children, although the term 'educate' is not always used in a formal sense. In addition, educators of young children also care for them.

Although every effort has been made to keep the language simple and uncluttered by jargon, inevitably some words have been used that may be unfamiliar to some readers. A glossary has been included to clarify some of the terms used in the text.

Many of the exercises suggest that you discuss your thoughts and ideas with a 'colleague or supervisor'. Some early years workers work alone and do not have easy access to a colleague or supervisor. An appropriate person to discuss your work with may be a college tutor, a health visitor or a foster carers support worker. It may also be possible to get involved in any local groups or networks if you are a foster carer or childminder, and to find colleagues within these with whom you could share your work.

In general, this book is meant to be read as a whole. Good practice in early years care and education is hard to compartmentalize and there is a certain amount of crossover between the contents of the chapters. However, it can be used to 'dip in' if there are particular issues you wish to look into more fully.

1 The Role of Good Practice in Early Years Care and Education

INTRODUCTION

Good practice in childcare and education is a concept that you may have many ideas and thoughts about already. On a daily basis, the majority of early years practitioners will incorporate good practice into the care and education of children without a great deal of consideration about what exactly it is you are aiming to achieve. Maintaining safety standards, tackling discrimination and working positively with parents are some examples of the sorts of good practice activities that many early years practitioners take for granted as part of their role. So, why read a book on good practice in early years care and education? For some readers the goal will be to try to organize and expand their ideas about good practice, in order to work towards a qualification – perhaps a *National Vocational Qualification (NVQ)*. Others may have recognized that recent developments in childcare and education, such as the expansion of integrated services, have brought the question of quality provision to the forefront of debates about early years service provision.

Childcare and education practices are not static; they vary between and within different cultures and change over time. In order to raise standards, early years practitioners need to develop skills to question different practices and approaches and to instigate change. Learning about good practice is an essential tool in the process of developing high-quality services in the range of childcare and education settings.

Principles and Values

Values are about the standards or attributes which a culture, society or individual holds as being important or desirable. Many values are reflected in the laws of the society by which they are held to be important. For example, in western society, it is generally believed that human life is valuable, and this is reflected in laws that place heavy penalties on murderers. Values are general statements about how a society functions and as such, they do not reflect how we might behave in all situations. Different values may conflict at times, presenting us with moral or ethical dilemmas. For example, although killing others is not generally considered acceptable behaviour in western society, exceptions are made in the cases of war, self-defence and possibly 'mercy killings'. In some cases where individuals have helped suffering friends and relatives to die prematurely, the legal penalties have been light and there has been considerable public sympathy for the people involved. Although we value human life in western society, we also value the right to avoid suffering, and sometimes these two values can conflict.

Principles are more detailed statements about standards and expectations, which may provide a clearer guideline for behaviour. For example, NVQ standards give a detailed account of the principles of good practice in childcare and education. Such principles are based on values within the wider society. They may also reflect current issues within a particular sector of society.

Values guide our behaviour, but do not always help us make decisions in all circumstances. Most ethical dilemmas have no easy answers and many require careful negotiation, tact, diplomacy and creativity to find a solution that will satisfy those involved without compromising standards. In childcare and education, the rights of the child (see Chapter 2) and the rights of the parent can sometimes come into conflict, as can the rights of different children. For example, some Muslim communities in British society have expressed a wish that their children should be educated separately from non-Muslim children. This may be because schools in the UK promote Protestant Christianity as the main form of religion. Some Muslim communities believe that their children would be better off in separate schools where their religion is taught and the cultural values of their community are maintained.

Some may argue that this situation would be discriminatory, and would widen existing divisions within society. Others might argue that different cultural and religious groups have the right to ensure that their own religion is promoted to their children within the educational context.

Think — *A Chance to Think*

Ethical dilemmas arise in situations where our values are challenged or different sets of values conflict. These situations can be very stressful and hard to resolve, particularly where strong feelings come into play.

Exercise 1

Read the following case study and answer the questions below. Compare your answers with the sample answers in the Appendix.

AMY

Amy's father complained that his child had been hit several times by another child at nursery. Amy had received bruising to the face during the last attack and her father was extremely angry. The other child, Sam, had learning difficulties that involved some problems with controlling impulses. Sam had been in nursery only for a short while and was still finding the environment bewildering and hostile at times. Sometimes the other children teased him or made comments about him. Amy's father had expressed the view that 'handicapped children' should be educated separately on several occasions. Staff at the nursery were concerned that this situation could escalate.

1 Write down the conflicting principles or values in this case.
2 Whose rights might you need to support in this situation?
3 What steps could you take to try to improve this situation and whom would you involve?

One of the most difficult situations for early years practitioners can be where the interests of the child and parent conflict. For example, when parents are not able to provide adequate care for their children it may be that alternative forms of care may be sought, perhaps by the social services. The parents' needs to live with their children may be overridden by the children's needs to be properly cared for. In this case, the law (Children Act 1989) establishes the principle that in all such situations, the child's welfare should be paramount. The law acts as a guideline in this particular case, but not all principles and values relating to childcare are embodied within it.

Values and principles help us to make decisions about different courses of action, and provide guidance on standards and expectations in terms of the type and style of childcare and education offered. However, they do not give us detailed guidance on specific situations and how to deal with these. Many issues that arise in childcare and education settings cannot be predicted or prepared for. Early years practitioners need to develop an understanding of the range of issues that may be at stake and develop skills in understanding and applying sometimes conflicting principles in a range of situations. Early years practitioners also need to develop their own value systems through reflective practice (as outlined in Chapter 9).

Principles of Good Practice in Early Years Care and Education

You may well be asking the question 'How do we decide what is and is not good practice in childcare and education?' Good practice is determined by the expectations of children, parents and early years workers in the context of the wider society. These expectations will be based on what is considered acceptable practice at this point in time and in this culture. However, some principles may be harder to establish and less easy to agree on. For example, few would argue with the principle of physical safety for children in any childcare and education setting, but the ways in which early years practitioners try to establish anti-discriminatory practice may excite a wider range of responses as exemplified in Exercise 1.

Early years workers may also ask 'Why do we need principles of good practice?' if so much good practice is common sense. Principles of good practice offer guidelines for planning and delivering high quality services to children. They offer a baseline standard from which to develop high quality care. They also offer a basis of comparison so we can measure or assess improvements over time and understand that good practice is a developing concept.

Think · A Chance to Think

In order to raise and maintain high standards in childcare and education, the principles of good practice should underpin the practical activities that early years workers are involved in on a day-to-day basis. This does not mean that you should have to pause and consider the principles underpinning every single task. However, it does mean developing an awareness of the relevant issues and ensuring that this awareness guides the work you do.

For example, child sexual abuse has been identified as a significant social problem in societies across the world in recent years. One of the ways in which professionals and parents can try to prevent such abuse is to help vulnerable children to identify when adult behaviour is unacceptable. Part of this type of work with children is to help them understand about personal privacy and their rights in respect of their own bodies. Working this way with children can help build confidence and a clear sense of acceptable and non-acceptable behaviour in others. Early years practitioners have a role in encouraging this sense of privacy and separateness in children by treating them with respect and sensitivity during personal care. Children can be encouraged to perform personal tasks for themselves and to develop a sense of boundaries in terms of how others touch and hold their bodies.

1 Write down a list of five or six practical childcare and education tasks that you might do everyday.
2 Taking each task in turn, try to make a note of the relevant good practice issues and how these might influence the way in which you perform the task.
3 Discuss your ideas with a colleague or friend.

5

Principles of good practice in childcare and education are often written down. They may be included in policy documents such as equal opportunities policies, NVQ statements of underlying principles, statements of organizational aims or other written communications such as charters. The National Children's Bureau is one of the many organizations working with children which make a statement of their values and principles. Many workplaces will have such written materials reflecting the standards of care and the expectations that parents and others can have of the quality and style of childcare and education offered. As previously stated, some principles are considered to be so essential that they are part of the law. For example, Health and Safety regulations enforce standards of physical safety in all work settings.

Principles of good practice may be imposed by external agencies responsible for maintaining standards, for example OFSTED. Some standards are set by outside bodies, such as the National Childminding Association (NCMA) and CACHE (Council for Awards in Children's Care and Education). Written statements of principles are important because they act as a reminder of what is expected. However, they are not a substitute for thinking and learning about good practice, developing our own views and actively working towards higher standards for the children we care for.

Development of Good Practice

Early years practice is not the same as it used to be! How we care for and educate children changes over time and varies between different cultural settings and societies. Many of the childcare practices of the early twentieth century or even the 1980s would not be acceptable now. For example, it was common in western societies in the past to send children to bed without dinner as a punishment. As an early years practitioner today, you would probably consider depriving a child of nourishment as an unacceptable form of punishment. Young babies used to be swaddled – wrapped tightly in cloths so that their limbs were more or less immobilized – a practice which modern day childcarers would not consider.

Childcare and education practices tend to reflect the norms and values of society at a particular point in time. As these norms and values develop and change, practices will also change to reflect them. This process is not a neatly organized adoption of new practices and standards, but often involves lengthy and sometimes acrimonious debates between proponents of different schools of thought on a particular issue. For example, smacking used to be a standard punishment for the majority of children in British society, and for many children this is still the case. However, in recent years the anti-smacking lobby has become increasingly active in trying to outlaw smacking, claiming that it is a humiliating form of punishment that is ineffective and in breach of the rights of the child. Some would like to see smacking made illegal as it is in a number of other countries. Others argue that parents should have the right to punish their children as they see fit, and that smacking is effective and necessary in some cases. State instructions have adopted anti-smacking policies for all early years practitioners and settings.

Exercise 3

Think of some of the childcare practices of the past and make a list of those that are no longer seen as acceptable today. Write down your thoughts on why these practices might have changed over time. Discuss your ideas with a colleague or friend and see if they have any different explanations for the changes. Look at the sample answers in the Appendix.

Childcare and education practices are also culturally relevant – they are part of the wider culture in which children are being brought up and so they reflect the values and norms of that culture. A current example is the age at which children start school. In Britain, children usually start school in the term in which they are 5. In other European countries, the USA and Australia, children do not begin their formal schooling until they are 6 or even 7 years old.

Cultural differences in childcare and education practices are an important issue in multicultural societies like Britain. Cultural norms and values vary between groups and individuals and childcare practices may also vary between different sections of society and individuals within those sectors. As any new parent knows, there are many different methods of performing the simplest childcare task and a great many firmly held views on each method. However, more fundamentally, different cultural groups within a society may well have significantly different childcare and education practices which may well result in early years practitioners sometimes experiencing situations where their own values and standards are in conflict with those of parents. Good practice in childcare and education involves developing sensitivity to and

6

awareness of other cultural values and norms and ensuring that all cultures are valued and recognized within the childcare setting, without compromising good quality care. This can be a difficult and demanding task, involving some dilemmas and many uncertainties about how to deal with difficult situations.

Role of the Early Years Practitioner in Promoting Good Practice

The role of the early years practitioner in promoting good practice is more demanding than simply following sets of guidelines about how to provide the best quality care. Although policies and guidelines are helpful in establishing baseline standards of care, and ensuring that early years workers understand what is expected of them, they do not deal with every contingency. Situations will arise where you will need to use your judgement and experience to make decisions on how to proceed. The role of the early years practitioner will therefore include the responsibility of developing good judgement and acquiring the necessary knowledge on which to base this judgement. This means that early years practitioners need to keep up to date with current ideas and trends in childcare and education, and to be aware of the debates going on in some areas of the sector.

Think

A Chance to Think

Knowledge and understanding of the relevant issues can help us make informed decisions about different courses of action and improve the standard of care and education offered. Early years practitioners need to learn about different cultures, lifestyles and family types in order to be able to meet the needs of all the children in their care.

Exercise 4

Read the case study below and answer the questions. Discuss your answers with a friend or colleague and then compare them with the sample answers in the Appendix.

SANDRA

Sandra had been in the reception class at school for one term and had settled well. In the second term, her teacher started a project which involved asking the children to bring in photos of themselves as babies, to make into a display. Sandra came home very distressed on that day and told her mum she was not going back to school again. Sandra knew that her family did not have any baby photos of her because she had been adopted when she was 4 and had been with her 'forever family' for only six months. She had seen all the photos that had come to her new family with her, and she knew none of them showed her as a baby. She also knew that no one had taken photos of her as a baby, because the social worker had asked her birth parents if any existed.

1 What issues does this case study raise about different types of families?
2 How could the project have been presented better?
3 Note the good practice issues that should have been considered when planning the project.
4 How could Sandra be helped to recover her confidence and enjoy the project?

Good practice is changing over time, in line with changing social norms and values and improving standards. Much of good practice is contained in concepts such as equality of opportunity and children's rights. You need to have not only knowledge about relevant practices, policies and the law, but also the ability to ask questions or to seek information about particular situations that may arise. After all, you cannot be expected to know everything. However, it is important to know the limitations of your own knowledge and to be able to evaluate your own strengths and weaknesses. In order to implement good practice you need to think and reflect as well as act. This ability to evaluate our own contributions and improve them through planned change is called reflective practice and it is fully explored in Chapter 9. As an early years practitioner committed to raising standards it is important to seek training and development, use staff appraisal opportunities if available and become part of the monitoring and review procedures connected with your work.

Checklist of Good Practice Issues

- Know the policies and guidelines relevant to your work and work within them.
- Be aware of the legal framework for childcare and education and how this impacts on your role.
- Extend your own learning where possible and be aware that we all need to learn.
- Reflect on your own work and consider how this might be improved.
- Question practices in your work setting that you feel need improving.
- Reflect on your own views on other cultures and different lifestyles and how these can be valued in your work setting.
- Consider how children's rights are promoted in your work setting.
- Participate in staff training and development where possible.
- Try to become involved in monitoring and review procedures in your work setting and make use of any appraisal system to evaluate your own contribution.

Limitations on Good Practice

Good practice in childcare and education is not just a matter of good intentions. In order to ensure that standards are high, resources need to be committed to ensuring that staff have appropriate training and development, that appropriate physical resources are available and that there are good management and support structures. Budgets do not always seem adequate to meet the various demands made on them. However, it is also easy to blame budget restrictions for the inadequacies within a particular work setting, without looking further to see if other deficiencies are also a problem. Anti-discriminatory practice is not just about activities and displays celebrating the highlights of a range of cultures. It is also about the day-to-day manner and attitude of the staff towards the children and their families and the ways in which this reflects interest in and respect for their different cultural and religious backgrounds.

A Chance to Think

Not all organizations actively promote good practice in all areas of work. You may find yourself in a setting where there is only 'lip-service' paid to implementing policies or other principles of good practice or where there is a culture of tokenism towards important issues like equality of opportunity and anti-discriminatory practice. Often this stems from a lack of understanding of the issues involved and their impact on the children and their families.

Exercise 5

Read the case study below and answer the questions. Compare your answers to the sample answers in the Appendix.

ROSE STREET NURSERY

Rose Street is a privately owned nursery established in an increasingly affluent area of a large town. All the staff are white, but some of the children are from British Asian families, who have recently moved into this previously mainly white area. Some of the white parents have been heard to make comments about the neighbourhood starting to attract the 'wrong sort'. You overhear a colleague talking to a white parent, who comments, in relation to two Asian children standing close by, 'They get everywhere, don't they?' Your colleague laughs and seems to agree with the parent. Later you mention this interchange to the manager. She does not seem to think there is a problem unless the children actually overheard the conversation. She points out that the other member of staff has been in the job for many years and although she thinks equal opportunities issues are 'a lot of rubbish', she is a very experienced worker who provides good care for the children.

1 Do you agree with the manager that the practitioner probably provides good care to all the children at the nursery for whom she is responsible? Explain your answer.
2 To what extent do you agree with the manager that there is a problem only if the children actually overheard the conversation? Explain your answer.
3 What sort of response to the comment would have been more appropriate?
4 What measures would you consider necessary (if any) to improve standards of childcare in this nursery and who would they involve?

Although resource restraints have their place in limiting the growth of good practice, the attitudes and values of early years workers are also significant. Not all workplaces show commitment to good practice. This lack of commitment usually stems from the top down and is reflected in lack of staff training, lack of policies or policies which are not actively implemented and lack of self-awareness about good practice issues among staff and managers. Such organizations can be self-perpetuating as new staff adopt the practices of existing staff and staff who may argue for change become frustrated and leave.

Malik (1998) states that 'Staff development, training, monitoring and review are essential in supporting good practice because good practice never stops. It is a continuous process of learning and gaining new experiences' (p. 66).

Links with Training and Qualifications

Standards of good practice are an essential part of the current training and qualifications structure for childcare in the UK. The NVQ/SVQ (Scottish Vocational Qualification) standards explicitly state the principles of good practice which the candidate is expected to demonstrate during assessment. Other qualification courses either implicitly or explicitly include good practice as part of the criteria for assessment. Students on any early years programme are expected to explore and understand issues of good practice, including the values inherent within these and the methods by which good practice can be practised in day-to-day activities with children and contact with parents and families.

REFERENCES AND FURTHER READING

Donnellan, C. (ed.) (1992) *Children's Rights: Issues for the Nineties, Vol. 13*. Cambridge: Independence Educational.

Franklin, B. (ed.) (1995) *The Handbook of Children's Rights: Comparative Policy and Practice*. London and New York: Routledge.

Malik, H. (1998) *A Practical Guide to Equal Opportunities*. Cheltenham: Stanley Thornes.

Millam, R. (1996) *Anti-Discriminatory Practice: A Guide for Workers in Childcare and Education*. London: Cassell.

Moss, P. and Pence, A. (eds) (1994) *Valuing Quality in Early Childhood Services: New Approaches to Defining Quality*. London: Paul Chapman.

Pugh, G. (ed.) (2001) *Contemporary Issues in the Early Years: Working Collaboratively for Children* (3rd edn). London: Paul Chapman, in association with the National Children's Bureau.

2 Children's Welfare, Children's Rights

INTRODUCTION

This chapter deals with the support and promotion of children's welfare and children's rights in early years care and education. Children lack rights in almost every sphere of their lives, both private and public, reflecting the view that they are too immature to make rational, informed and competent decisions for themselves. But in denying children the rights that adults take for granted, we not only underline their dependency on the goodwill of adults, but also make them vulnerable to abuse, neglect and exploitation. Some would argue that not only does this lack of rights make children vulnerable, but also children may have much more ability to contribute to decisions about their own life and circumstances than is generally accepted.

The concept of children's rights is closely linked to the promotion of children's welfare. In order to ensure that children's rights are upheld, their welfare must be promoted across all aspects of their growth and development. The UN Convention on the Rights of the Child, adopted in 1989, makes a principled statement about the rights of children around the world, reflecting an increased awareness of the vulnerable position many children are in.

In this chapter, we shall explore the concepts of children's welfare and children's rights and look at how they are promoted in early years care and education. The legal position and legal rights of children will be discussed, as will the notion of 'the welfare of the child' within the law. Specific issues relating to the welfare of the child will be examined, including warmth, responsiveness, methods of control and communication. More specific issues relating to the rights and welfare of children from groups who are subject to discrimination will be explored in Chapters 3 and 4.

UN Convention on the Rights of the Child

The UN Convention on the Rights of the Child is a statement of principles about the way in which children should be treated and how their welfare should be promoted. The underpinning values of the Convention include the belief that children have equal rights to adults and that adults have a responsibility to ensure that children's rights and welfare are safeguarded and promoted. However, children do not have equal rights to adults in British society. They do not have full citizenship or the same legal status as adults, and young children are both vulnerable to, and dependent on, adults. As such, children's rights differ from adult's rights and are dependent on adult support for their existence.

Children are in a strange position in some respects. They depend on adults for their care and safety and this dependent status makes them vulnerable. Children, especially young children, do not have a voice of their own and, therefore, rely on adults to promote their welfare. But who decides what is best for a child or children? Decisions about a child may well reflect the interests or beliefs of adults, without the child's own particular feelings and concerns being taken into account at all.

The UN Convention addresses this issue by stating the principle that 'In all actions concerning children . . . the best interests of the child shall be a primary consideration' (Article 3.1). Basically, decisions about children and how they should be treated should, in theory, be based on some disinterested view of what is best for them. Sadly, we know that this is not always the case.

The Convention deals primarily with the public domain of childcare, outlining other major principles in relation to the rights of children. The Convention states that children should have the right to have their own views and wishes listened to and taken into account, in terms of any decision-making about them. Children's age and stage of development will influence how much weight their views are given. The extent to which the child's views are acted upon should not influence the fact that the child's views should always be respected.

The Convention includes the principle that all children have a right to survival and development, and that resources should be committed to ensuring this is the case. The concept of development used is holistic, referring to all aspects of a child's development.

Finally, the Convention includes the principle that all children have these rights, whatever their status, culture, gender or level of ability. This principle is a statement that all children should have equality in terms of their basic rights.

The Convention includes sections that deal with the ways in which these principles can be put into practice, and how children's rights can be supported legally, politically and economically. The resourcing, promotion, monitoring and review of children's rights are discussed. One of the ways in which the Convention suggests that children's rights can be safeguarded and promoted is through the education of childcare practitioners in terms of understanding and acting upon these principles.

Development of Rights for Children

Children's rights have not always been taken seriously. Not so long ago, the concept of children having rights of their own had little credibility. Children may have, in some senses, been considered to have rights that were conferred via their parents, who had the power to determine what these might be and to uphold them or not as they saw fit. The belief that adults always know what is best for children and always act in their best interests made specific rights for children seem superfluous. The child, in many ways, was seen as the property of her parents. They could make decisions for her and about her without any reference to her wishes and feelings. But now:

Instead of being dismissed as 'utopian nonsense' or mere 'political correctness' the idea that children possess rights which adults should respect and help to promote now informs aspects of government policy and legislation, the policy of voluntary sector and charitable organisations as well as the practice of welfare professionals.

(Franklin, 2002:3)

But how has this concept of children's rights grown and developed validity?

Many of the principles of children's rights have gradually developed from increasing knowledge and understanding of the vulnerability of children and the abuses and hardships they suffer from. Every day, thousands of children across the world die of starvation, are subject to abuse and neglect, lack parents, warmth, shelter, love and even basic care. Many children are suffering from the effects and privations of war, from living as refugees or in such abject poverty that their basic needs are not met. Other children live in virtual slavery, work in appalling conditions and are denied access to education, basic health care and security. In some cases, children are subject to adult exploitation for money, sexual gratification or power.

It is clear that in many cases, the belief that adults can and will confer rights on their children simply cannot always be upheld. In discussing some of the well-known child death inquiries of the 1980s (Jasmine Beckford, Kimberley Carlile and Tyra Henry), Franklin states:

These high profile cases also exploded the myth of the family as an institution which offered its members security and safety; for children, and also for women, the family was a potentially dangerous arena. (1995: 4)

The lobby for children's rights is diverse and includes politicians, policy-makers and professionals involved in the education and care of children. Their common belief is that the condition of children will not be improved unless they have legally and politically supported rights, conferred upon them directly and backed by adequate resources. To some extent, the concept of children's rights has now become a 'legitimate claim' and is enshrined in British law and some areas of policy. But the debate continues while, as a society, we vacillate between concepts of children as vulnerable beings in need of protection and concepts of children as potentially or actually dangerous or out of control, and therefore requiring fewer rights and more restrictions.

Meanwhile, according to Franklin (2002:2):

One in three children lives in poverty (Bradshaw, 2002:2). 26 per cent of recorded rape victims are children, 4,000 children are placed on child protection registers each year, and more than 40,000 children a year are killed or injured in road accidents . . . 20 per cent of children and adolescents in the UK suffer some form of mental health problem, 75 per cent of looked after children leave school without any formal qualifications, African-Caribbean children are six times more likely to be excluded from school than other children, half of all disabled children and their families live in unsuitable accommodation.

Children Act 1989

The main piece of legislation supporting the rights of children in the UK is the Children Act 1989, which incorporates some of the concepts and principles of children's rights as conceptualized in the UN Convention. In particular, the Children Act is based on the principle that the child's welfare is 'paramount'. The term 'paramount' refers to the idea that the child's welfare should be the focus of deliberations, and the main consideration, when making legal decisions about any aspect of the child's life or circumstances. It does not mean that the child's welfare will be the only consideration, just that it should be the main and most important one.

The Children Act changed how the roles of both the state and parents were seen in relation to children, by moving away from the principle that children were passive, defenceless beings for whom it was legitimate to make decisions on their behalf. The Act recognized children as participants in decisions about their own welfare and acknowledged that children's views of what would contribute to their welfare might differ from the views of both their parents and the welfare services.

The Children Act made it a duty for welfare services and the courts to establish the child's wishes and feelings in respect of any legal decisions to be made about the child and to take these views into account when making those decisions. Children's age, stage of development and level of understanding are significant in determining the extent to which their views influence the decision-making process about their life and circumstances. The Act does not specify or give guidelines about the extent to which the child's views should count: therefore, in theory and practice, the child's views could be ascertained, considered and then ignored.

The provisions of the Children Act mainly affect children who come into contact with the courts because of family breakdown, care proceedings or other court processes within which decisions about the child's life are to be made. However, the Children Act made a significant general change to the legal status of children, which affects all families. Prior to the Act, parents were deemed to have 'parental rights' over their children. These formed the legal basis on which the relationship between parents and children rested. The Act removed the notion of 'parental rights' and replaced it with that of 'parental responsibility'. This change was introduced to get away from the idea that parents had rights over children and the connotations of ownership inherent within this, and to introduce the idea that parents have responsibilities towards their children in terms of their welfare.

The Children Act is the first piece of legislation in the UK which specifically focuses on the rights of children and which tries to ensure that children are viewed as active participants in their own welfare, rather than objects to be acted upon. The Act is a step forward, but it has limitations, not the least for young children, who are so often seen as not having the age and understanding to participate in decisions to be made about them.

Policy and the Rights of Young Children

The rights of all young children to high quality care and education have long been neglected in the UK, in contrast to many other European countries where affordable, high quality early years care and education are the norm. However, the development of central policy in the early years has finally been established. Since 1998, the National Childcare Strategy has been driving change in the field of early years care and education. The growth of separate care and education services across a range of providers including social services, education, and the independent and voluntary sectors had led to 'a patchwork of fragmented and uncoordinated services, showing wide variations between one part of the country and another' (Pugh, 2001:10). Lack of coordination between diverse services with differing aims and standards had resulted in a complex and confused range of services which often failed to meet the real needs of young children and their families. For example, a working parent may have placed a 2-year-old in private daycare. As the child reached 3, the parent may have wanted the child to attend a school nursery in order to access free pre-school education. This may have seemed particularly important in situations where the nursery class was in the school that the parents hoped the child would attend or where older siblings attended. The social and educational benefits of such a move seem clear, until you realize that in order to access the half-day session in school nursery, the child must leave private daycare and that other arrangements would have to be made for the other part of the day.

Childcare and education provision had grown in a fragmented and uncoordinated fashion, without reference to either the needs of children or the steadily growing increase in numbers of women working. Access to services varied and depended on economic status, with poorer children less likely to be in high quality childcare and very narrow choices of places in some areas. Many children simply could not get a pre-school place.

Lack of a central strategy and low levels of funding meant that early years care and education services often did not reach the children most in need of support. The National Childcare Strategy was introduced to improve the number of early years places available; to improve the quality of early years care and education; to develop the early years workforce in terms of quality and quantity; and to develop new services to children and families that met their needs more effectively. The strategy was linked to policies encouraging women back into the workforce; improving educational standards for all children; promoting social inclusion and the reduction of child poverty.

Meeting the needs of children and parents requires increased flexibility and this includes the development of 'wrap-around' services providing nursery grant-funded education and day care on the same premises. The development of Early Years Centres of Excellence to model good practice promoted new approaches to meeting the needs of working parents in particular.

In addition to the development of Early Years Development and Childcare Partnerships to promote the goals of the National Childcare Strategy at local level, many local authorities have established Early Years Services to address issues across care and education.

Alexander (1995) suggests that there are five principles on which Early Years Services should be established, rooted in the concept of children's rights:

- Children come first.
- Children have a right to be recognized as people with views and interests.
- Children should have the opportunity to be part of a family and community.
- Parents, carers and communities need to be supported in promoting the interests and the welfare of their children.
- Children have the right to safe play environments.

Alexander argues that Early Years Services may not achieve their goals unless they base them on the concept of children's rights and make these rights central to the planning, provision and standard setting in early years care and education.

The development of coordinated and flexible services has started to transform opportunities for young children and their families. In addition to those already discussed, the raft of initiatives includes:

- Places for all 3- and 4-year-olds as part of the National Childcare Strategy.
- The Foundation Stage curriculum (QCA, 2000).
- 'Birth to Three Matters' (Sure Start, 2002).
- Financial support for parents who want to work.
- National inspection service through OFSTED's Early Years Directorate.
- Sure Start projects to support children under 4 and their families in the most socially and economically deprived communities.

However, there are still many anomalies in levels of provision, access, cost and choice depending on location and income.

Efforts to bring together early years services across traditional divides have been hampered by existing structures and professional differences. Moss (1999) suggests that the government has missed an opportunity to completely re-think early years services and to make more radical and far-reaching changes. Despite many positive developments in some areas, some barriers to progress remain:

- different professional interests, pay and training structures of those involved in working in early years (teachers, childcare assistants, nursery staff, playworkers, childminders)
- problems in breaking down departmental structures to provide a genuinely holistic service to children (many early years services are based in local authority education departments)
- resourcing
- ensuring that quality is even across the range of educare options parents can choose from.

The Green Paper 'Every Child Matters' (DfES, 2003), published in response to Lord Laming's report on the inquiry into the circumstances leading to the death of Victoria Climbie, sets out sweeping proposals for change designed to further integrate services for children and to improve standards and quality for all. The Green Paper outlines five outcomes for children:

- Being healthy
- Staying safe
- Enjoying and achieving
- Making a positive contribution
- Economic well-being.

In order to achieve this, the government is 'for the first time ever requiring local authorities to bring together in one place under one person services for children' (DfES, 2003:2). This proposed integration of services is the next step in recognizing and meeting children's holistic needs through coordinated services, and goes some way further in sweeping away traditional divisions between care and education. Specific proposals include:

- Creating Sure Start Children's Centres in the 20 per cent most deprived neighbourhoods.
- Promoting full service extended schools, including health and social care support services.
- Increasing out of school activities through a Young People's Fund.
- Expanding the Child and Adolescent Mental Health Services (CAMHS).
- Improving speech and language therapies.
- Tackling homelessness.
- Reforms to the youth justice system.

Action is focused on four areas:

- Supporting parents and carers.
- Early intervention and effective protection.
- Accountability and integration.
- Workforce reform.

A key element in these plans is to bring together children's social services and local authority education under a single Director of Children's Services, with plans to develop Children's Trusts in all local authorities to include education, social, health and other services for children.

Clearly, these proposals are designed to support children's rights through properly coordinated and integrated services to meet the whole range of their needs. The extent to which these initiatives are successful will depend on the ability of professionals and organizations to break down existing divides and ways of working and to develop new approaches to and understandings of young children's needs and how best to meet them.

Promoting Children's Rights and Welfare

Children's rights need to be promoted at all levels in order to be effectively upheld. In the previous section, the role of the State in promoting children's rights through policy development has been discussed. In this section, the role of settings and individual early years practitioners in promoting children's rights and welfare will be explored.

Early years settings have a responsibility to promote children's rights in a number of ways, determined by guidelines and legislation. Depending on the type of service or setting, these could include:

- Complying with requirements of curriculum guidelines, e.g. Foundation Stage (QCA, 2000); 'Birth to Three Matters' (Sure Start, 2002).
- Complying with quality standards for inspection and regulation detailed in the National Standards for Under Eight's Daycare and Childminding (DfES, 2001).

The notion of young children's rights is enshrined within such guidelines and legislation, providing a clear structure for settings or services to work within. For example, the Curriculum Guidance for the Foundation Stage for 3–5-year-olds sets out principles of good practice on which the work of the setting should be based. These principles uphold children's rights to equality; inclusion; high quality care relating to all aspects of development; and high standards of pedagogy. 'Birth to Three Matters' sets standards for settings to follow when working with the youngest children. The National Standards for Under Eight's Daycare and Childminding (DfES, 2001) provide a basis for registration and inspection of all types of care settings, setting out 14 standards against which quality is measured (Baldock, 2001). There is a more detailed discussion of quality standards for early years settings in Chapter 5.

Implicitly within such principles there is an emphasis on the relationships developed between individual early years practitioners and the children.

Early years workers have a responsibility to promote the rights and welfare of the children they care for, within the limitations of their job role. One of the principles of good practice in early years work is that the welfare of the child should be 'paramount' and that the rights of the child should be upheld and promoted. But what does this mean in practice? In some senses it means putting the best interests of children first in all our work with them. But how do we determine what the child's best interests are?

One of the ways we can look at the child's welfare is in terms of the developmental outcomes for the child. Various studies show that there are a number of different aspects of interaction between carers and children, which have an influence on their development. The most important dimensions of interaction between carers and children are summarized by Bee (2000), drawing on a wide range of studies. They are:

- warmth
- responsiveness
- methods of control
- communication.

The different ways that carers interact with children within these dimensions can have an influence on the child's development and behaviour. These are not the only factors affecting a child's welfare. Other influences on welfare are explored in other chapters of this book.

Warmth and Responsiveness

Defining 'warmth' is difficult, but we all probably know the difference between a warm and a cold or hostile approach to a child when we observe it. Bee (2000: 380) draws on Maccoby's (1980) work to suggest that:

A warm parent cares about the child, expresses affection, frequently or regularly puts the child's needs first, shows enthusiasm for the child's activities, and responds sensitively and empathically to the child's feelings.

Expressing warmth in educare settings is a crucial element of promoting the child's welfare. Elfer (1996, p. 30) states that most early years workers agree that 'warm and responsive relationships are of great importance in supporting children's learning and development'. However, Elfer reports that in practice such relationships do not appear to exist.

Clearly, there is progress to be made in further developing good practice in this area. Warmth in interactions with carers is linked to good levels of security, high self-esteem, responsiveness to others, empathy and altruism in children. Other studies show that low warmth or hostility to children is linked with insecurity and low self-esteem.

In a follow-up study on children who had been physically abused before the age of 5, it was found that the outcomes were poorer for both the children who had been abused and the control group of non-abused children who lived in households lower on warmth and higher on criticism. Poor outcomes included depression, behavioural problems and making and keeping friends (Gibbons *et al.* (1995) in Department of Health (1995)).

Warmth means liking children and wanting to be with them, and showing this. In some ways, it is difficult to teach practitioners how to be warm, as it is an intuitive dimension that early years practitioners bring to their care of children. However, there are a number of points to consider when expressing warmth to children in your care:

- All children should be treated warmly.
- Difficult behaviour in a child should not change the levels of warmth they receive.
- Warmth needs to be genuine and frequently expressed.
- Warmth can be shown through having knowledge of the child's individual concerns and preoccupations and expressing interest in these.

Responsiveness is the ability to tune in to the child's needs and wants, moods and problems and to respond to them. A responsive adult will be sensitive to the child and aware of her. Responsiveness is linked to cognitive and language development, social competence and compliance with adult requests (Bee 2000).

Katz (1998) argues that children need to have genuine experiences in order to reach optimum development. Genuine behaviour by early years practitioners is important in terms of expressing warmth and being responsive, not least because children are sensitive and know the difference between real and false expressions. For example, it is important to avoid blanket praise of children's work ('Very nice dear, just put it over there') and instead, spend a little time discussing the work in more detail.

Developing an environment that promotes respect and positive interactions between individuals is an important outcome of showing warmth and being responsive. For example, Marsh (1994) cited in Woods (1998, p. 210):

commends nurseries where there is a general climate of respect in the interactions among children, among adults and between children and adults, and where all individuals treat others and are themselves treated with respect and courtesy.

Think) A Chance to Think

Expressing warmth and being responsive to every child can be difficult at times. Some children may at times seem more attractive, responsive and affectionate to you than others. Adult interactions with children are not just based on the adult's behaviour. The child's behaviour and responses will be significant in the interactions. It is a two-way process, involving feedback between adult and child to build a relationship, which (it is hoped) is based on warmth and mutual respect. However, as the adult you have responsibility to promote this process and to try to resolve any difficulties in building a relationship with a child, by being responsive to the child's needs.

Exercise 1

Read the following case study and answer the questions below. Compare your answers with the sample answers in the Appendix.

PAULA

Paula is 3 years old and has just started in the nursery class at the local school. Before this, she was in a private day nursery. Her parents have placed Paula with you for childminding. You pick her up from school at 11.30 a.m. and care for her until 5.00 p.m. Paula usually gets upset before she has left the school gates. She whines and cries about minor upsets or imagined problems. She is apathetic in the house and does not want to get involved with the activities you do with the other child you mind, who is 4. She never wants to go to the park or anywhere out of the house and you have had some conflict trying to get her ready to go. During the introductory meetings you felt that Paula's unresponsive behaviour was probably due to the change in her care provision and that it would improve with time. Five weeks later you are starting to think you have made a mistake in accepting her, as she remains miserable and unresponsive and you do not feel you have built a relationship with her.

1 What steps could you take to try to build a warmer relationship with Paula?
2 How would you involve her parents?
3 How would you involve the nursery staff?

Methods of Control

One of the debates in childcare is whether smacking should continue to be a legally accepted method of control of children. In many other countries, particularly in Scandinavia, smacking is outlawed and parents are open to legal proceedings if they smack. In Britain, smacking is still legal, but under attack from campaigners who want to see smacking stopped. The Newsons' (DoH, 1995) study found that 81 per cent of parents hit their children, although 'about half thought they should not' (Newson, 1969). In the 1960s, 95 per cent of parents in the Newsons' survey hit their children and 80 per cent thought this was right. Smith *et al.* (1995) found that 91 per cent of children in their study were hit, including about three-quarters of children under 1 year. They also found that 'Smacking was the commonest form of punishment, in terms of the number of children who had experienced it' (DoH 1995: 12). The organization EPOCH (End Physical Punishment of Children) argues that smacking children is a fundamental breach of their rights as people.

Smith *et al.* (1995) also looked at other punishments and concluded most importantly that 'Most punishments were used by parents who were generally warm and supportive' (DoH 1995: 85). The context of punishment seems to be significant in that punishment appears to be most effective where children also received rewards and praise.

Bee (2000) found the following significant factors in successful approaches to controlling children:

- consistency of rules
- high expectations of children in terms of mature behaviour
- moderate restrictiveness (neither too restrictive or too permissive)
- mild punishments that come early in a sequence of behaviour, delivered with minimum emotion.

In early years settings in the UK, smacking is not used as a punishment. This has not always been the case, but the anti-smacking lobby, the growth of support for children's rights and the development of child-centred methods of care and education have outlawed smacking in educare settings.

The area of control of children is one of the most important in terms of promoting children's welfare and upholding their rights. In dealing with unwanted behaviour, it is all too easy for adults to show negative power over children and to 'win' at the expense of the child's self-esteem and dignity. Children inevitably show unwanted behaviour for a whole range of reasons. These can include:

- tiredness
- stress or unhappiness, not necessarily caused by factors in the immediate environment
- jealousy, competition for attention with other children
- attention-seeking behaviour
- tantrums related to the child's developmental stage
- boredom, inability to concentrate on some occasions
- experimentation with boundaries as part of maturation
- frustration, lack of confidence in learning new skills
- conflict within the group of children.

Reducing the incidence of unwanted behaviour can be achieved by

- being warm and responsive to the child
- explaining rules within the child's level of understanding
- being sensitive to difficult times such as when the child is tired or hungry
- giving each child special attention and individual responses
- showing approval and giving praise
- being consistent and fair
- setting boundaries and being firm in maintaining them.

Despite your best efforts, unwanted behaviour will occur as children struggle to make sense of the world around them. In dealing with unwanted behaviour the following factors should be borne in mind:

- The child's behaviour may be disapproved of, but not the child herself.
- A calm, controlled manner will support the child's dignity and your own.
- Sanctions should be mild, immediate and enforced.
- Explain why the behaviour is unacceptable in terms the child can understand.
- Do not respond in a way that will humiliate the child, or use sarcasm to the child.
- Ignoring some attention-seeking behaviour may be appropriate, but only if no one is getting hurt or upset.
- When it's over it's over! Give the child positive attention and affection to re-establish rapport when his unwanted behaviour has stopped.
- Shouting may be effective in the short term, but sooner or later you will have to shout louder and, as you model this behaviour, the child may shout back.

It is important to discuss issues of control with parents, emphasizing that you will not use physical punishment whatever they do at home. Working together with parents will reinforce your chances of achieving good levels of control with a child while maintaining the child's welfare and well-being. Discussing effective, supportive control methods with parents may, in some cases, help them to move to better practices in this area which support the child's health and development in a positive way. Parents may also have information and advice for you, which will help you with good practice in achieving control with their child.

Think A Chance to Think

The control of children in your care is one of the most important areas in which to develop good practice. No one is always consistent in terms of appropriate sanctions and calm, authoritative responses to unwanted behaviour, but achieving a balance of 'firm, but warm' in most incidents will be an important step in supporting the welfare of the child.

Exercise 2

Read the short case study and answer the questions below. Compare your answers with the sample answers in the Appendix or discuss with a colleague or supervisor.

NATHAN

Nathan is 4. He has been in your nursery class for two months since moving to the area with his mother, after his parents separated. Nathan is a lively child, with an enquiring mind, but a fairly short span of concentration. He does not settle easily to tasks and walks around the room, sometimes disrupting other children. Occasionally he gets into conflicts with other children, in which he gets very angry and upset, shouting abuse and sometimes hitting. Nathan can be attention seeking at times and some of the conflicts with other children seem to be based on jealousy, because the other child has been getting attention. Staff are starting to describe Nathan as a problem.

1 What positive steps could you take to reduce the incidents of unwanted behaviour from Nathan?
2 How would you deal with his outbursts as a team?
3 What would you need to discuss with Nathan's mother?

Communicating with and Listening to Children

Perhaps one of the most fundamental ways of securing children's rights and putting their welfare first is to listen to what children have to say about their own needs and wishes. It is all too common for adults to assume that they know best in terms of children's needs, but there is an increasing body of evidence which suggests that children can contribute sensibly and effectively to debates about their own welfare. The Children Act 1989 states that children's views should be ascertained and taken into account when legal decisions are being made about their welfare. But for children in their everyday lives, there may not be such an emphasis on finding out what they think about the quality of their care and education.

In Denmark, the right of children to be listened to is one of the principles laid down by the Ministry of Social Affairs (responsible at national level for all early childhood services). The ministry states:

It must be emphasized that children should be included in the planning and execution of activities in daytime child care facilities, according to their age and maturity, and that children in this way are able to gain experience of the connection between influence and responsibility on a personal and social level.

(Danish Ministry of Social Affairs 1990: ch. 2, cited by Langsted in Moss and Pence 1994)

The Children as Citizens Project was set up to ensure that children were heard on the various aspects of their everyday life, 'to strengthen children's right and opportunities to say things that will be heard and to which importance will be attached'. Emphasis was placed on children having the information to contribute to decision-making, within a framework of work methods which allowed for their contribution. In one part of the project, children in the kindergarten aged 3–6 were given the right to make decisions about their life in the kindergarten, after older children had done a study on how the staff 'trampled on' the younger children's rights. Changes made included giving the young children open choice about when they ate, played outside and had a drink.

Listening to young children has to be done sensitively and with consideration of the different ways in which children communicate. It is easy for adults to question children in ways that assume certain answers and do not give children time and space to express their thoughts and feelings in their own way. All too frequently adults put words in children's mouths such as 'You do like that don't you?' The Danish project highlights the fact that it is possible for quite young children to express view and opinions, if there is a will to listen to them.

There are a number of possible barriers to listening to children about their own welfare. These might include:

- adult fear of loss of power
- belief that the children would make irrational, unfeasible decisions
- resource implications
- parents' views and feelings
- time investments
- belief that children are better off if adults decide things for them.

The benefits of listening to children's views and opinions on how they should be cared for include:

- a better service, more matched to meeting children's needs
- less conflict between adults and children about keeping to rules
- children learning social responsibility and informed decision-making processes at an early age
- positive impact on the children's social, emotional, cognitive and language development of taking part in this process
- preparing children for the responsibilities of citizenship
- providing a rich new source of information on how adults can best contribute to child welfare.

Listening and talking to children in our day-to-day dealings with them is an important factor in their cognitive, language, emotional and social development. Children gain enormously from discussions with adults in which their views and opinions are attended to, responded to, taken seriously and acted upon. Taking time to let young children struggle to explain a difficult point to you can sometimes feel like a luxury in a busy educare environment. To the child it may be a step forward in their knowledge of the world around them and an important stage in understanding and using new language.

(Think) **A Chance to Think**

Listening skills are crucial to getting feedback on the views and opinions of children in your care, but it is surprisingly common for adults simply not to listen properly to the things children have to say.

Exercise 3

Look at the list below and think about whether and how often you do any of these non-listening activities:

- interrupting when others are talking
- finishing sentences for others
- not paying attention, for example, no eye contact, being distracted, doing another task

- assuming you know what you are about to be told
- being too busy to listen
- giving unwanted advice as soon as someone starts to tell you a problem
- not making opportunities for others to talk to you.

(adapted from Kay 2003: 74)

Draw up a plan of how you could get feedback and ideas from children in your workplace or placement on one aspect of the activities they are involved in. Describe the listening skills you might need in order to put your plan into action and the sort of information the children would need in advance to contribute informed views and opinions. Discuss the way in which you would present your proposals to other staff and parents, in order to get their support. Share your ideas with a supervisor, colleague or tutor and compare them with the suggestions in the Appendix.

Increasingly, older children in particular are being listened to in a range of educare settings. Pupil councils are established in some schools, offering the chance for children to contribute to rule-making and other decisions. The right of young children to have their say in what will contribute to their welfare is not established in the UK as yet. In the meanwhile, listening to individual and groups of children and being sensitive and responsive to their needs will contribute to keeping their best interests to the fore.

Conclusions

This chapter has dealt with mostly general issues about children's rights and children's welfare in the social and political context. The importance of supporting children's rights is reflected in their vulnerability and uncertain legal status. Like all of us, children respond best to positive, supportive relationships in which they are valued and respected. In order to reach optimum development, children need adults to promote their welfare in their interactions with them and to ensure that their rights are upheld. Early years workers have a particular responsibility to model good practice in this area and to create environments where children can be treated well. The rights and welfare of particular groups of children who may suffer inequalities of treatment in the wider social context and in care and education will be explored in Chapters 3 and 4.

REFERENCES AND FURTHER READING

Alexander, G. (1995) 'Children's rights in their early years', in Franklin (1995).

Baldock, P. (2001) *Regulating Early Years Services*. London: David Fulton.

Bee, H. (2000) *The Developing Child* (9th edn). Needham Heights, MA: Allyn and Bacon.

Bradshaw, J. (2000) 'Poverty: The Outcomes for Children', *Children 5–16 Research Briefing No. 18*, July, London: ESCR.

DfES (2001) 'National Standards for Under Eight's Daycare and Childminding.'

DfES (2003) 'Every Child Matters.' (summary)

Department of Health (DoH) (1995) *Child Protection: Messages from Research*. London: HMSO.

Donnellan, C. (ed.) (1992) *Children's Rights: Issues for the Nineties, Vol. 13*. Cambridge: Independence Educational.

Elfer, P. (1996) 'Building intimacy in relationships with young children in nurseries', *Early Years*, **16**, 30–4.

Franklin, B. (ed.) (1995) *The Handbook of Children's Rights: Comparative Policy and Practice*. London and New York: Routledge.

Franklin, B. (ed.) (2002) *The New Handbook of Children's Rights – Comparative Policy and Practice*. London and New York: Routledge.

Gibbons, J., Gallagher, B., Bell, C. and Gordon, D. (1995) *Development after Physical Abuse in Early Childhood: A Follow-up Study of Children on Protection Registers*. London: HMSO.

Katz, L. G. (1998) 'Introduction: what is basic for young children?', in S. Smidt (ed.) *The Early Years: A Reader*. London: Routledge.

Kay, J. (2003) *Protecting Children: A Practical Guide* (2nd edn). London: Continuum.

Langsted, O. (1994) 'Looking at quality from the child's perspective', in Moss and Pence, (1994).

Maccoby, E. E. (1980) *Social Development: Psychological Growth and the Parent–Child Relationship*. New York: Harcourt Brace Jovanovich.

Marsh, C. (1994) 'People matter: the role of adults in providing a quality learning environment for the early years', in L. Abbott and R. Rodger (eds) *Quality Education in the Early Years*. Buckingham: OU Press.

Moss, P. (1999) 'Renewed Hopes and Lost Opportunities: Early Childhood in the Early Years of Labour', *Cambridge Journal of Education, Vol. 29, No. 2*

Moss, P. and Pence, A. (eds) (1994) *Valuing Quality in Early Childhood Services*. London: Paul Chapman.

Newson, J. and E. (1969) *Patterns of Infant Care*. London: David Fulton.

Pugh, G. (ed.) (2001) *Contemporary Issues in the Early Years* (3rd edn). London: Paul Chapman.

QCA (2000) 'Curriculum Guidance for the Foundation Stage.'

Smith, M., Bee, P., Heverin, A. and Nobes, G. (1995) *Parental Control within the Family: The Nature and Extent of Parental Violence Towards Children*. Thomas Coram Research Unit, University of London, in DoH (1995).

Stainton Rogers, W. and Roche, J. (1994) *Children's Welfare and Children's Rights: A Practical Guide to the Law*. London: Hodder and Stoughton.

Sure Start (2002) 'Birth to Three Matters.'

Woods, M. (1998) 'Early Childhood Education in Pre-school Settings', J. Taylor, and M. Woods (eds) (1998) *Early Childhood Studies*. London: Arnold.

3 Equal Opportunities and Anti-Discriminatory Practice

INTRODUCTION

Equal opportunities policies are central statements in early years settings about the standards of care and education that children and their families should expect to receive within the framework of equal opportunities legislation and early years quality standards and curriculum guidance. They provide a basis for developing good practice in terms of meeting the range and diversity of children's needs. Equality of opportunity does not mean that all children should be treated in the same way. It would hardly be equal to offer the same level of support to an able-bodied 4-year-old, who is advanced in her development, and a child of the same age who has profound learning disabilities. Some children and families will need a great deal more support than others to access the care and educational opportunities available to them. Different children and families will also need different types of support depending on their specific needs. For example, a child and her family may need language support to access nursery provision whereas another child may need financial support in order to gain access to the early years services he needs.

Equality of opportunity depends on each child being valued in terms of gender, family background, race, culture, religion, type of family and ability. If children are not valued as individuals this may act as a barrier to them achieving their full potential by accessing care and education services.

Anti-discriminatory practice is about the development of ways of working which promote equality of opportunity and avoid discrimination (different or unequal treatment) between different children and their families. It includes not behaving in a discriminatory way, and also actively supporting children and their families to try to overcome the impact of discrimination in other areas of their lives. Anti-discriminatory practice in early years contexts tends to focus on how early years practitioners behave towards children and their families while in the workplace. However, anti-discriminatory practice is not just about how we try to behave. Understanding the roots of discrimination and the way that prejudice can influence our behaviour in subtle but powerful ways can help to develop the attitudes and beliefs that are an essential part of anti-discriminatory practice.

There are many misleading views about what anti-discriminatory practice actually means and how early years practitioners can achieve good practice in this area. Occasionally, it can seem that anti-discriminatory practice is about race issues alone, ignoring the other bases of discrimination in our society. Or that anti-discriminatory practice simply means 'treating everyone the same', when in fact not all children and families have the same needs.

You may feel unsure about discussing anti-discriminatory practice and equal opportunities issues. Millam (1996, p. 2) gives several reasons as to why discussing anti-discriminatory practice can feel uncomfortable:

- lack of understanding of the issues and terminology
- do not feel it is appropriate to discuss this issue with small children
- worried about 'getting it wrong' or upsetting people
- do not know where or how to start tackling these issues
- worried about addressing own attitudes and prejudices.

All of these are valid reasons for being concerned about addressing these issues. But early years practitioners need to get involved in promoting equal opportunities through anti-discriminatory practice, in order to raise standards for all children in their care and provide them with a safe, pleasant environment in which to grow and learn.

There are no simple definitions of anti-discriminatory practice or easy routes to achieving good standards in this area. In a social system where discrimination exists in so many public and private areas, achieving complete lack of discrimination is probably impossible. Early years practitioners have a responsibility to work with children to minimize discrimination, not only for the benefit of the children, but also because of the great influence that practitioners may have on the thinking and belief systems of the next generation of adults.

This chapter explores the theoretical and legal framework for promoting equality of opportunity and anti-discriminatory practice in British society. This includes the bases of discrimination, the ways in which discrimination is manifested and the impact of discriminatory behaviour on individuals and groups. The legislative framework will be discussed in terms of the effectiveness and limitations of the law in promoting and supporting anti-discriminatory practice. The value of policy statements in early years settings will also be discussed. Chapter 4 explores how anti-discriminatory practice can be developed in early years settings by promoting equality of opportunity for children and their families and challenging discriminatory attitudes and behaviour among early years practitioners, families and the children themselves.

In both chapters there are a number of terms that may be unfamiliar to some readers. These are defined more fully in the glossary at the end of the book.

There are many different beliefs about what anti-discriminatory practice is or could be. Some people have quite limited views about the range and scope of discrimination in society and sadly, some dismiss anti-discriminatory practice altogether. Perhaps others have positive intentions, but a poor understanding of the issues and how to put anti-discriminatory practice into action, resulting in an avoidance of the issue as it may seem full of potential pitfalls. In other early years settings, anti-discriminatory practice is well understood and work practices reflect a commitment to improving standards in this area of practice.

33

Exercise 1

Ask other early years practitioners, supervisors, colleagues and tutors what they believe anti-discriminatory practice to be and make a note of the answers. Does everyone have similar views on this? Do you agree with all the views expressed? From your discussions with others and your own reading and reflection, try to form a personal view of anti-discriminatory practice and what it means to you. Discuss this view with colleagues, supervisors and tutors and ask for their comments. This is a difficult and controversial area to study, especially if you have been subject to discrimination personally or have family or friends who have been discriminated against. Or you may have views and feelings which are described as 'prejudiced' in the literature or on courses you have attended. If you feel this is a particularly difficult topic, try to find a mentor to discuss your feelings about the issues and to give you support in your studies.

The Bases of Discrimination

Prejudice, Discrimination and Negative Stereotypes

Discrimination is based on prejudice, which quite simply means 'pre-judging', making assumptions about others. But where do these assumptions come from and why are they applied to particular groups and individuals? Prejudice is based on negative stereotypes of others. A stereotype is a fixed view or image of a group of people, based on perceived characteristics of that group, which may be exaggerated or simply incorrect. For example, in the author's training sessions on anti-discriminatory practice, white students have responded to the brainstorm trigger 'Asian people' with 'corner shops' and 'curry' almost without fail. The students were describing stereotypes (not necessarily their own) of Asian people, which are common in British society.

Stereotypes are persistent mental images, which may be very resistant to change. Studies have shown that individuals will maintain their stereotypes in the face of facts that prove them to be incorrect. Individuals also select information about others which reinforces our stereotypes of them, while ignoring information which does not fit into that fixed mental image. For example, in a training session a student expressed strong views that 'immigrants' (a term he used for all black and Asian people) took all the local jobs leaving white people unemployed. When asked what proportion of the population of the area he thought was non-white, he suggested about 40 per cent. When shown statistics that demonstrated that the non-white population in the area was 1.6 per cent and that unemployment in the area ran at about 2 per cent, he flatly refused to acknowledge this could be the real situation.

Stereotypes are applied indiscriminately to all those who are perceived as part of a particular group, whether that individual possesses those particular characteristics or behaviours or not. This process is sometimes described as 'labelling'. Stereotypes can be positive or negative, but it is negative stereotypes that form the basis of prejudice.

Prejudice, based on negative stereotypes of others, is an attitude or feeling which is often expressed as negative views of an individual or group. Prejudices vary between different social groups and can change over time, but individual prejudices tend to be influenced by the wider culture.

Prejudice alone, although unpleasant, is not necessarily damaging to individuals or groups. Holding a view or opinion of others will not impact on those others unless it is translated into behaviour. Discrimination is unequal or negative behaviour towards others rooted in prejudices, which are based on negative stereotypes. Discrimination is therefore about behaviour. Anti-discriminatory practice is about behaving in a way that excludes discrimination and actively seeks to reduce the impact of discrimination on the lives of others.

Not all groups of people are subject to prejudice. In western societies, the main groups who suffer discrimination, based on prejudice, are:

- cultural and ethnic minorities
- people with disabilities
- women and girls
- gays and lesbians
- older people.

Other groups who are sometimes perceived in negative terms and may be subject to discrimination are travellers and New Age travellers. This list is certainly not exhaustive.

Theories about Prejudice

There are many theories as to why certain groups become the subjects of discrimination, some of them based on notions of the way in which the socialization of children reinforces the norms and values of the dominant culture at the expense of other cultures. Socialization is the process by which children absorb the attitudes, values, expectations and beliefs of the wider culture from parents especially, but also from their peers, teachers, early years practitioners and others portrayed in the media. These cultural norms and values give children many messages about what and who is valued in their social system.

Children learn that certain groups and individuals are treated and viewed differently in society and certain behaviours are considered more valuable than others are. They can absorb prejudices along with other cultural messages. For example, children may see that two-parent, heterosexual families are portrayed favourably in the media and that other types of families are seen as less valuable. Children's preferences in relation to toys and types of play have been found to be determined by their gender (Pitcher and Schultz, 1983). Children have no inherent predisposition to develop play within the boundaries of male and female gender roles, but they do respond to the often subtle but pervasive expectations of those around them.

Children will also copy and model the behaviour of those around them, particularly parents and other adults who are powerful in their lives. If children observe adults behaving in discriminatory ways, they may well copy these. For example, negative comments about children with disabilities or children from different cultural backgrounds may well be reproductions of parental behaviour.

Absorbing cultural messages is part of the way in which children become part of their own social system and this is an important process in itself. But children will absorb negative messages about others along with other information and this can perpetuate the negative stereotypes and prejudices on which discrimination is based. Prejudices are more apparent in some cultures rather than others.

The process of socialization may explain to some extent how prejudices and discriminatory behaviour are perpetuated in a social system, but does not explain why some groups became subject to discrimination in the first place.

Certain aspects of prejudice are rooted in history, such as some of the discriminatory beliefs about black people, and beliefs about gender differences between men and women on which stereotypes are based.

One theory, which was used to try to explain the behaviour of the Nazis towards Jews in the Second World War, is that individuals have different types of personality based on the parenting style they experienced as children. Prejudice is thought to be more likely in those with authoritarian personalities – individuals who experienced a very strict parenting style as children. This theory may help to explain different levels of prejudice between different individuals, but it does not really explain where prejudice comes from initially.

Stereotypes are often reinforced through the media, such as notions of 'femininity' and 'masculinity' and caricatures or negative stereotypes of gays and lesbians, black and Asian people. Stereotypes can be created and reinforced, for example, the hysterical 'gay plague' and 'judgement of God' reporting on HIV and AIDS in the 1980s which was linked with an upturn of homophobic attitudes and discrimination against gays.

Discrimination in Practice

Discrimination appears in many different disguises. Although there are laws that restrict discrimination on the basis of race, gender and disability (but not sexuality or age), discrimination is often hard to identify and prove. Discriminatory behaviour can be direct (overt) or indirect (covert). An example of overt discrimination would be to put a notice on a pub door saying 'No Travellers' or to scrawl 'Go home Pakis' on a wall. Direct discrimination includes racial attacks, harassment, denying access to a person with a disability or making assumptions about an individual's capability on the basis of their gender. An example of covert discrimination would be to choose a male candidate for a job over a similarly qualified female candidate, because you believe the female candidate may cost your firm money by having children and requiring paid maternity leave. However, in this case you would give other reasons for choosing the male.

Some acts of discrimination are institutionalized, in that they are built into the structures and procedures of a particular body or organization. For example, workplaces which emphasize 'presenteeism', requiring workers to be on the premises for long hours and equating these long hours with commitment to the job, may well discriminate against parents, particularly women, who have child-care responsibilities. Jobs that are traditionally dominated by a mainly male or mainly female workforce may be difficult to access by the opposite gender. For example, early years work in the UK continues to be dominated by women, reflecting social and cultural norms in western societies (and possibly the low rates of pay in some early years job roles). Males who aspire to work in childcare may have their motives treated with suspicion or may simply not feel comfortable in an all-female environment.

Changes are taking place all the time in terms of discriminatory practice, particularly in employment. In 2000, in line with European Court rulings, the armed forces in the UK have had to abolish their ban on gay and lesbian recruits. Prior to this, any serving recruit suspected of being homosexual was investigated and if proof was found, expelled summarily from their post. However, discrimination is still widespread, affecting many individuals in their work and social lives and in their right to live free from harassment. The much-publicized

Stephen Lawrence case highlighted the ongoing incidence of harassment and attacks which many non-white people are subject to, sometimes on a daily basis.

The importance of knowing and understanding the basis and incidence of discrimination in UK society helps us to understand the discriminatory experiences that some children live with on a day-to-day basis.

Discrimination and Disability

Disability is defined as a limitation on activity which goes beyond the normal range, which is long term and which affects everyday activity. There is a myriad of different types of disability, but it is important to recognize disability in terms of the impact it has on an individual's day-to-day life rather than by applying labels, which describe medical conditions. Until the last century disabled people were usually 'treated' by being institutionalized as children or when parents were no longer able to care for them. Many disabled people lived their whole lives in institutions, unable to enjoy many of the freedoms and pleasures of life that others took for granted. Others were denied access to education and employment, the chance to make relationships, to travel and to live independently. The labels used to describe people with disabilities confirmed their unequal status in society, for example sub-normal, retarded, deficient. The introduction of policies which promote care in the community have gradually changed the way in which people with disability are treated and now many people who would have been institutionalized in the 1960s live independently. A National Children's Home report in 1995 showed that 98 per cent of disabled children now live with their families (Hobart and Frankel 1999).

Parallel to this change in policy has been a change in the way people with disabilities are seen. The medical model of disability, which prevailed until relatively recently, emphasized the illness or cause of disability and whether it could be treated or not. In cases where treatment was not indicated, the disabled person was often institutionalized and their potential for independence in some areas lost. Disabled people were often described in terms of their disability and stereotyped accordingly. The social model of disability emphasizes the need for social attitudes and values to change in order to promote equality for disabled people, arguing that the real cause of problems for disabled people is the attitudes and prejudices of those around them.

Discrimination and Racism

The concept of race is based on perceived differences between groups of people, according to their appearance. This often focuses on skin colour in white-dominated societies.

The concept of race as a way of distinguishing between different groups of people is now largely discredited. It is generally believed that there are no significant distinctions between different groups and that humans are all of one race. The concept of race merely provides a basis for discrimination and is usually allied to some form of differentiation between people. Dividing people by race based on perceptions of skin colour is not only a flawed concept but is also impossible to achieve as the numbers of people with complex mixed heritages increases. However, the term 'racism' is still used to describe behaviour that is discriminatory on the basis of perceptions of difference in race.

Considering differences in ethnicity may be a more useful way of recognizing diversity. Ethnicity relates to the customs, cultures, beliefs and norms of different groups. Everyone has an ethnic group, whatever their background. However, the term ethnic minority is commonly applied to groups whose cultural background varies from the mainstream culture within a society. Individuals who are part of ethnic majorities tend to be less aware of their ethnicity because they are less obvious within society as their culture is dominant.

Racism has been a social issue in British society for many years despite legislation to curb discrimination on the grounds of race. It takes the form of individual and group behaviour in communities, including social exclusion of non-white people, racist abuse, attacks and threats. Racism is also part of British institutions, denying non-white people access to jobs, political power, education and training opportunities and housing. White ethnocentrism dominates British culture, denying people from ethnic minorities the right to follow their own cultural practices and beliefs freely, without harassment and discrimination. Until relatively recently there were few non-white people on television or in the media and few positive images of different cultures and ethnic groups. Multiculturalism is now promoted in all early years settings, but racism continues to invade all aspects of the lives of many children and their families. A study by Milner (1983) demonstrated that children as young as 3 are able to understand the meaning of colour differences between individuals and to perceive that being white is considered better than being non-white.

Discrimination and Gender

'Gender role' is the term used to describe the different behaviour associated with males and females in a social system. Gender roles are socially constructed, not biological, therefore they differ between different societies and change over time. Children learn their gender roles at an early age as part of their socialization into the family and wider culture.

Kohlberg (1987) found that children acquired a stable concept of gender at about five years old, but that they understood gender differences at an earlier stage. Children absorbed the concept of their own gender as part of their cognitive development and developed in accordance with that concept. Other theories of gender development emphasize social learning, where children model themselves on the behaviour of others and modify their behaviour according to the approval or disapproval of those around them. A whole range of studies support the view that gender specific behaviour is reinforced by adult interactions with children, with different expectations of and different attitudes to boys and girls. Boys tend to be expected to be more robust and competitive and to be involved in more physical play. Girls are given positive feedback for being quieter, and better behaved and passive.

Stereotypes of males and females based on perceived gender roles can be extremely damaging to individuals in terms of reaching their full potential. Despite their relatively good educational performance, females still fail to obtain the best paid jobs and reach the same heights of promotion as males. Children may absorb messages about what girls and boys do and don't do at an early age as reflected in gender-specific play in early years. Discrimination against women is illegal in many areas, but continues to affect many women, particularly in education and employment.

Think A Chance to Think

Gender differences in play and other behaviour can go unnoticed because they are so embedded in the behaviour and attitudes of the wider culture. Children are often discouraged from playing across the gender divide by the responses of other adults and children. For example, a boy of 3 enjoyed wearing nail varnish when he joined in with his older sisters, who played at 'being grown up'. However, when he started at school in his fifth year, he stopped wearing nail varnish because 'boys don't do that'. He had absorbed another element of gender-divided behaviour.

Exercise 2

Over a period of several days, keep a diary or record of examples of gender-specific play or behaviour in your placement or work setting. Record any examples of the ways in which gender differences are reinforced by adults or children, such as comments like 'Boys don't do that' or 'You'll make a lovely mum' in response to a girl pretending to make lunch for a family. Share your observations with a colleague or friend.

Discrimination and Children

Children live in the real world and not a protected 'bubble' of childhood. Young children are in the most formative period, learning from everything around them (Sylva and Lunt, 1982). From the earliest years they absorb the views and opinions of others and the messages about the world around them, which they get from their families, other people, television, videos and books (Tassoni and Beith, 1999). Along with all the other information they receive and try to make sense of, children absorb the negative stereotypes and labels, which are part of the dominant culture in their society. Children will apply these stereotypes to themselves if they are part of a group that is subject to prejudice. Children may absorb feelings of inferiority because they are from an ethnic minority, disabled, or from a family background that does not conform to cultural norms. For example, there is currently a debate about the types of families that should be promoted in schools, which heavily emphasizes the normality and rightness of two-parent, heterosexual nuclear families. Children from different types of families may suffer as they compare their own situation and are compared with this 'norm'.

The Impact of Discrimination

Discrimination has an impact on every aspect of an individual's life chances. Children from some groups will suffer in terms of education and employment chances, health, housing and income, because discrimination has exerted a complex and negative influence on their lives. Children may be affected directly by discrimination in terms of their learning and development. Tassoni (1998, p. 11) suggests the following list of effects of discrimination:

- The effects are lifelong.
- Children may not reach their full potential.
- Low self-esteem may have a negative impact on the child's ability to form relationships.
- Children may have lack of confidence to experiment.
- Children may feel ashamed of their race or culture.
- Children may internalize negative views and feel as if they deserve poor treatment.

For example, African Caribbean children consistently do less well in school than any other group, resulting in poorer chances of accessing further and higher education and the type of employment that goes with better qualifications. The Swann Report (DES, 1985) found that one of the contributory factors to this situation was the low expectations teachers had of black children.

Children who absorb negative messages about themselves from the world around them on the basis of perceptions of their ethnicity, culture or level of ability, or any other factor, will often develop a low level of self-esteem and a poor self-image. Children may become aware of their perceived 'difference' and respond to it by failing to achieve their individual potential.

For example, children from minority cultural backgrounds may gradually become aware that their cultural norms and values are not valued in the wider world, or even that they are derided and dismissed by members of the dominant culture. How many times have we heard adults arguing that members of minority cultures do not have a right to continue their own religious and cultural practices, or even speak their own language, while living in 'British society'?

Recent debates about how notions of the family should be taught in schools, mentioned above, have emphasized heterosexual, two-parent families as the norm. Presumably the children of single-parent families and lesbian and gay couples should therefore consider themselves as living in 'abnormal' families? Studies have shown that adopted children are happy with their status and generally do well in their families. However, most do not want their adopted status discussed at school because it may be used as a basis for bullying.

Discrimination has a complex impact on children, which is not always easy to understand but may include:

- the development of negative self-perception and low self-esteem
- failure to achieve full potential in learning because of low expectations of self
- failure to achieve because of the low expectations of others impacting on self-image
- poorer social relationships, lack of confidence
- low aspirations and lack of ambition
- feelings of shame, inadequacy and anger
- 'acting out' and poor behaviour, which may influence achievement.

Think   *A Chance to Think*
_____

Expressing cultural norms and beliefs is something we take for granted if we are part of the dominant culture in a society. Images of the dominant culture are reflected in the media and in the lives of others around us. But for those of us who are part of a minority culture, expressing cultural beliefs and norms can be a struggle as others fail to recognize the value of different cultures or appreciate the importance of each individual's right to express themselves in line with their own values.

Think about the ways in which you express your own cultural norms on a day-to-day basis. For example, the clothes you wear, the food you eat, the way you express any religious or spiritual feelings, the relationships and interactions you have with family and friends. Now try to imagine being in a place where none of your behaviour is acceptable and where you are mocked or threatened by others for your appearance, the language you speak and the values you hold. Some of you will not need to imagine this as you may well have had personal experiences of discriminatory behaviour, based on perceptions of your ethnicity, sexuality or other bases of discrimination.

How does it feel? What sort of response would you like to make to a society which treated you in this way? Consider that for many children and their families this is a day-to-day reality. What would be the long-term impact on individuals subjected to this type of discrimination? Discuss your thoughts with a colleague or supervisor.

Legislative Framework for Anti-Discriminatory Practice

There are a number of laws in the UK which support anti-discriminatory practice in many areas, including childcare and education, by making some types of discrimination illegal. The law does not apply to all bases of discrimination, nor protect all groups and individuals against discrimination. It is important to remember that not all discriminatory practice is illegal in the UK. For example, there are many age restrictions in employment, including a compulsory retirement age of 65 years old in many jobs.

The law does not prevent all discriminatory practice. Despite the legislation, racist attacks persist, women have yet to crack the so-called 'glass ceiling' of higher management jobs, and inequalities in access to health, housing, employment, education and training and other services persist.

However, despite some limitations, the law does provide a basis for anti-discriminatory practice in some areas and it can give access to redress for some individuals and groups who have experienced discrimination. Perhaps just as importantly, the principles of anti-discrimination and equality of opportunity which underpin the legislation give a clear direction for policy development in this area.

All early years practitioners need to be aware of the legal requirements and how they may influence the work with children and families. The principles underlying equal opportunities legislation are an important basis for understanding how to develop better standards of anti-discriminatory practice.

Some legislation lays down general principles of equality. The UN Convention on the Rights of the Child 1989 is not a law, but many pieces of legislation are based on the articles within it, many of which relate to anti-discriminatory practice and equality for all. The Human Rights Act 1998 sets out a series of rights, based on the European Convention on Human Rights, which must be upheld within the law. These include the right to education as well as the 'prohibition of discrimination'. Other legislation directly related to early years care and education is based on principles of equality and anti-discriminatory practice. The Care Standards Act 2000 establishes OFSTED's Early Years Directorate as the body responsible for registration and inspections of all daycare and childminding settings, and sets out minimum standards for these settings. Standard 9 relates to requirements on settings to promote equal opportunities for all and Standard 10 relates to requirements to provide for and meet the needs of children with special educational needs.

Equal Opportunities Legislation and Gender

The Sex Discrimination Acts of 1975 and 1976 effectively outlaw discrimination on the basis of gender in the areas of employment, housing, education and other services. The Equal Opportunities Commission was set up to ensure that allegations of discrimination on the grounds of gender are investigated and to monitor cases brought under the Act. The Equal Pay Act 1970 made it illegal to pay men and women different wages for the same type of work. Before the Equal Pay and Sex Discrimination Acts, it was perfectly legal to pay men and women differently for the same work. Men's wages were often considered more important than women's wages because men were seen (and still are sometimes) as the sole breadwinners in families.

The Acts distinguish between direct and indirect gender discrimination, acknowledging that some types of discrimination are not easily identified or challenged. For example, jobs that provide conditions less favourable to part-time workers (predominantly women) may discriminate indirectly against women.

In childcare and education services, it is very important to ensure that children are not discriminated against on the grounds of gender. In the mid-1970s, when the Sex Discrimination Acts were passed, girls generally did not do so well in school as boys in terms of educational achievements. Studies showed that boys received more positive attention from teachers and that there were higher expectations of boys. In the intervening years, girls have overtaken boys in nearly all areas of educational achievement, reflecting attempts to redress the balance and offer girls the same standards in education as boys received.

Outcomes of attempts to restrict sex discrimination in early years settings

- The same curriculum for boys and girls has been established in early years settings and both are encouraged to play across the range of toys and equipment.
- Early years establishments try to avoid gender discrimination in terms of toys, books and equipment within the setting, for example, books which only portray women in traditional female roles.
- It is illegal to discriminate between males and females in terms of recruitment, selection, promotion and remuneration in early years employment.
- Positive encouragement for girls to access areas of science and technology which were previously seen as predominantly male.

Race Relations Act 1976 and Race Relations (Amendment) Act 2000

The Race Relations Act 1976 replaced and extended previous legislation dating from 1965, which had started the process of outlawing discrimination on the basis of colour, race, nationality and ethnic origin in many areas of public and private life. The Race Relations (Amendment) Act 2000 extended the provisions of the Act to the police and other public bodies and gave a duty for major public bodies to eliminate unlawful racial discrimination and to promote equality. The Race Relations Act 1976 (Amendment) Regulations 2003 (the 'Race Regulations') amended the 1976 Act, including, among other provisions, a new definition of indirect discrimination and defining harassment on racial grounds as direct discrimination. The Commission for Racial Equality supports the Act in practice and can instigate proceedings where discrimination is identified. The law covers direct and indirect discrimination, but has some notable limitations:

- The Act does not exclude discrimination on the basis of religion or culture.
- The Act did not at the time create a separate category of law to deal with racial attacks.
- The Act does not influence racist attitudes and behaviour.

Examples of direct discrimination against individuals and groups on the grounds of ethnicity are, sadly, still plentiful. They include:

- remarks, taunts and name-calling
- harassment, threats and attacks
- negative assumptions about individuals and groups based on stereotypes
- employment discrimination by not employing members of certain ethnic groups.

Indirect discrimination may be much more common than we are aware of. Examples include:

- failure to meet the religious needs of certain ethnic groups, for example, opportunity for prayer, time off for festivals
- signs and instructions in the English language only
- eating arrangements and food which are unacceptable in some cultures.

Although the Act makes discrimination in employment illegal on the grounds of race and nationality, other evidence supports the view that covert discrimination in this area continues.

Outcomes of attempts to reduce discrimination on grounds of ethnicity in early years settings

- Positive images of non-white children in early years settings, such as books portraying ethnic minority families, black dolls, songs and stories from different cultural traditions, availability of different types of food.
- Acknowledgement and celebration of religious and cultural festivals and events from a wider range of cultures.
- Equal opportunities and anti-discriminatory practice are standard parts of early years courses.
- Promotion of multiculturalism in early years contexts among staff, children and parents.

Legislation and Disability

Prior to the Disability Discrimination Act 1995, there was very little legal support for people with disabilities in terms of ensuring anti-discriminatory practice, especially in the field of employment. Theoretically, under the Disabled Persons (Employment) Act 1944, firms and companies of a certain size were obliged to ensure that quotas of 3 per cent of the workforce were registered disabled, but in reality there was no enforcement of this requirement. The Disability Discrimination Act gives new rights to people with disabilities in terms of employment, access to goods and services and buying land or property. It also requires schools and colleges to provide information for people with disabilities. This includes information about how schools make arrangements for admitting pupils with disabilities, facilities and resources to ensure equal treatment of pupils with disabilities and access to educational opportunities on offer.

Successive Education Acts from 1944 onwards have supported the rights of disabled children and children with special needs to education with an increasing emphasis on integration where possible. The Education Acts of 1981 and 1993 introduced and extended the concept of special educational needs and the requirement that children with special needs should be assessed and monitored.

The Education Act 1996, part 4, defines a child with special educational needs and states that children with special educational needs should normally be educated within mainstream schools. The Special Educational Needs and Disability Discrimination Act 2001 became part 4 of the Disability Discrimination Act 1995 in 2001, making it illegal, among other things, for educational institutions to discriminate against disabled students. It also amended sections of the Education Act 1996 to make it unlawful for schools to discriminate against children on the grounds of special educational needs. Schools cannot refuse a place to a child who has SEN unless they can prove that admitting the child would adversely affect the education of other pupils or that they are unable to take the necessary steps to educate the child with SEN. LEAs are given a duty to offer advice and information to parents of children with SEN and to ensure there is a satisfactory system for resolving disputes and appeals between parents and the LEA.

The Code of Practice for Special Educational Needs 2001 protects the child's interests during the special needs assessment process, by ensuring that the child's needs are appropriately identified and met. This simply means that children with special needs have a legal right to good practice in identifying and responding to their educational needs. This right includes consultation with parents and other professionals, assessment, monitoring and review of the child's progress. There are five stages of assessment, culminating in statutory assessment and statementing. Most children have their needs met at the earlier stages because these involve focusing on individual children, planning and working in partnership to support their access to education.

Outcomes of attempts to increase disability awareness in childcare

- Emphasis on a policy of inclusivity, whereby children with special needs or disabilities are more likely to be placed and supported in mainstream early years settings.
- Emphasis on improving physical and psychological access to early years care and education for children with disabilities.
- Better support services, information and advice to families.
- Disability awareness training as a part of early years courses.
- Promotion of positive attitudes to disabled children and adults in early years settings.

Children Act 1989

The Children Act 1989 is not specifically an example of anti-discrimination law. However, as the major piece of legislation currently governing childcare in the UK, the underlying principles of the Act have a significant influence in this area. These include the following:

- The welfare of the child is paramount, regardless of the child's age, sex, religion, race or ability.
- The child's race, culture, religion and language must be taken into account when considering services, for example foster placements should reflect the child's cultural background.
- Local authorities have a duty to identify and offer support to children in need and their families (including a comprehensive assessment within the 'Framework for Assessment of Children in Need and their Families' (DoH, 2000).
- Local authorities must work in partnership with parents where possible to best meet the needs of the child.
- Childcare services have a duty to promote self esteem in children and support the development of their racial and cultural identity.

Other significant documents relating to the education and care of young children emphasize anti-discriminatory practice in all areas of work with children and families. Early years curricula (Foundation Stage and the National Curriculum Key Stage 1) are developed on anti-discriminatory principles, which support the concept of diversity through the curriculum content and delivery. For example, the Curriculum Guidance for the Foundation Stage (QCA, 2000) is based on a number of principles, one of which is that 'practitioners should ensure that all children feel included, secure and valued'. In order to achieve this, practitioners need to:
- Manage transitions effectively in partnership with parents.
- Develop trust and respect with children and families.
- Treat children as individuals to promote equal opportunities.
- Find out about children's home culture, faith, language and interests.
- Promote children's self-confidence as a key component of success regardless of their cultures and backgrounds.

The OFSTED registration and inspection standards (National Standards for Under Eight's Daycare and Childminding (DfES, 2001)) include a requirement that settings demonstrate that equal opportunities are supported for all children through anti-discriminatory practice.

Equal Opportunities Policies

Equal opportunities policies are found in the majority of early years settings contexts. Policies are developed to provide a framework for developing good practice in line with legal requirements. Policies generally make a statement of standards as regards the promotion of equality of opportunity in the workplace.

Sadly, in some settings, equal opportunities policies are written and then spend the rest of their lives gathering dust on a shelf until they are revised and a new version becomes the dust-trap! Like all guidelines, charters and policies, equal opportunities policies are valuable only if they are read, absorbed, discussed and used as a basis for developing higher standards of good practice.

 A Chance to Think

Equal opportunities policies can sometimes be seen as something that you have to have in order to meet the requirements of inspections and registration. In other settings, equal opportunities policies are working documents, which inform and guide the activities of the staff to reduce discriminatory work practices and highlight important issues in maintaining and increasing equality of opportunity in the setting.

Exercise 4

Read the equal opportunities policy in your workplace or placement and consider the following questions:

1 Were you given the equal opportunities policy to read when you started work/placement in the setting?
2 How was the purpose of the equal opportunities policy explained to you and were you given the impression that it was an important tool in improving good practice?
3 Who has access to the policy?
4 What sort of induction, training and ongoing discussions about equal opportunities take place in the workplace?

Discuss the answers you get to these questions with your supervisor or another appropriate person. Are there any improvements that could be made to the policy or how it is implemented in the workplace?

In order to make an equal opportunities policy a 'live issue' it must be implemented. Implementing an equal opportunities policy could include:

1 Ensuring that all early years practitioners in the setting have access to the existing policy and are aware of the contents.
2 Ensuring that parents and others should have access to the policy. For example, a short version (summary) could be displayed.
3 Students and new employees should be introduced to the policy as part of their induction.

4 All staff should be trained in terms of their responsibilities within equal opportunities legislation in general and their worksite policy specifically.

5 Revisions of the policy should be done in consultation with staff, parents and any other interested community representatives. Policy review should be regular and should be used to ensure policies are relevant and actively implemented.

6 Outcomes of the policy should be monitored and reviewed to chart the progress of raising standards in the work setting. This could include monitoring improvements in resources and equipment in terms of reflecting the cultural mix in the setting. It could include devising activities that promote cross-gender play and help girls and boys explore and enjoy toys and equipment they do not normally use.

7 Putting systems in place for ensuring change takes place.

With reference to the last point, one of the problems that has occurred in some areas is that equal opportunities policies do not always get implemented because responsibility for change is not clearly defined. Some organizations are moving towards equal opportunities targets or objectives as a way of more clearly defining expectations for change. The advantage of objectives or targets is that they are written in terms of what can be done, rather than in terms of sweeping generalizations or hopeful statements. Targets and objectives are usually small and manageable and are measurable so that the extent of change can be calculated more accurately. For example, an objective in the nursery could be to do an audit of resources and 'weed out' any that reflect discriminatory views and opinions (like books which persist in calling fire-fighters 'firemen' and showing all male characters). The responsibility for ensuring that targets and objectives are met is allocated when they are set, so it is clear who is doing what. Regular reviews ensure that targets and objectives are met and that new goals are set within a timescale of achievement. This approach is more dynamic and progressive and places the responsibility for change firmly within the setting. It is also useful for identifying resource deficits which are adversely affecting good practice in this area.

Think   *A Chance to Think*

Equality of opportunity is never fully achieved in a society which has so many bases of discrimination and where the lives of so many children and their families are affected by inequalities. Early years practitioners are permanently working towards better standards of anti-discriminatory practice in order to maximize the equality of opportunity of the children in their care. This task may seem overwhelming at times and it may seem that genuine change is hard to achieve. Or it may feel that everything has been done that can be done to promote equality of opportunity so far and no other steps are possible. Neither of these positions takes into account the real value of keeping the issue of anti-discriminatory practice alive through discussion, raising awareness and setting and achieving goals for change.

Exercise 5

Looking at every aspect of your workplace or placement, set a small number (about five) of small, achievable targets or objectives for change in order to further promote both equality of opportunity and anti-discriminatory practice. Consider who would be responsible for achieving the change and how it could be measured. Discuss your ideas with the appropriate person.

Conclusions

This chapter has set out the theoretical, legal and policy framework for promoting equality of opportunity in early years care and education through the continuing development of anti-discriminatory practice. Chapter 4 explores how this can be achieved in practice, by celebrating diversity and acknowledging and meeting the different needs of children in order to improve their access to early years services.

DES (1985) *Education for All*. The Report of the Committee of Enquiry into the education of children from ethnic minority groups, chaired by Lord Swann. London: HMSO.

Department of Health (DoH) (2000) *Framework for Assessment of Children in Need and their Families*. London: The Stationery Office.

Hobart, C. and Frankel, J. (1999) *Childminding: A Guide to Good Practice*. Cheltenham: Stanley Thornes.

Kohlberg, L. (1987) *Child Psychology and Childhood Education: A Cognitive-developmental View*. London: Longman.

Malik, H. (1998) *A Practical Guide to Equal Opportunities*. Cheltenham: Stanley Thornes.

Millam, R. (1996) *Anti-Discriminatory Practice: A Guide for Workers in Childcare and Education*. London: Cassell.

Milner, D. (1983) *Children and Race: Ten Years On*. London: Ward Lock Educational.

Pitcher, E. G. and Schultz, L. H. (1983) *Boys and Girls at Play: The Development of Sex Roles*. New York: Praeger.

Pugh, G. (ed.) (2001) *Contemporary Issues in the Early Years: Working Collaboratively for Children* (3rd edn). London: Paul Chapman, in association with the National Children's Bureau.

Sylva, K. and Lunt, I. (1982) *Child Development: A First Course*. Oxford: Blackwell.

Tassoni, P. (1998) *Child Care and Education*. Oxford: Heinemann.

Tassoni, P. and Beith, K. (1999) *Nursery Nursing: A Guide to Work in Early Years*. Oxford: Heinemann.

51

4 Promoting Equality and Diversity

INTRODUCTION

In Chapter 3 we looked at a theoretical framework for understanding the bases of discrimination, which affects some children and their families in British society. The impact of discrimination on children and the legal basis for anti-discriminatory practice were discussed. In this chapter, we shall look at practice issues in terms of promoting equality for all children and developing anti-discriminatory practice in your own work and in the wider context. Methods of developing new understandings of cultural diversity, children with disabilities and gender issues, and of dealing with our own and other's prejudices will be discussed, as will work practices aimed at promoting the self-esteem of all children. The multicultural approach is critically analysed and the differences between anti-discriminatory practice and multiculturalism assessed.

This chapter emphasizes practice issues with individual and groups of children who may experience discrimination in the wider social context. In theory, all children should be given equality of opportunity to develop their potential abilities to the maximum. Equality of opportunity is a complex goal, which is hard to achieve and may present the early years worker with dilemmas and difficulties. However, early years workers have a responsibility to work towards achieving the highest standards of equality of opportunity possible for the children in their care. In addition, early years workers also try to offset some of the discrimination some children experience in the wider world, by building self-esteem and valuing children for their individuality in the childcare setting. Developing equality of opportunity and anti-discriminatory practice in the workplace can involve early years workers in a whole range of work, covering any aspect of equality from teaching children about cultural and religious diversity, to dealing with racist attacks or bullying of children with disabilities.

In order to achieve good practice in this area, early years workers must have a solid basis of knowledge and understanding of the issues involved, as outlined in Chapter 3. You also need a range of practical skills. The following list covers the sorts of knowledge, skills and understanding that individual early years workers need to develop in order to promote equality in their work role:

- an understanding of the meaning of the terms 'equality of opportunity' and 'anti-discriminatory practice'
- an understanding of the link between stereotyping, prejudice and discrimination
- knowledge of the bases of discrimination in British society
- knowledge and understanding of the effects of discrimination on some children
- a belief that not all children have the same advantages
- a belief that to some extent you can make a difference to this
- skills in challenging adults and children who express discriminatory views about others
- skills in developing themes in your work which support all children's sense of individual value and uniqueness
- knowledge and understanding of cultures other than your own
- understanding of the impact of a range of disabilities on children's lives
- gender issues and the outcomes of gender bias in the early years
- knowledge of your own prejudices and ability to face and challenge these.

The list seems daunting, but the ability to work effectively in this area can be built up over time as you gather information and develop skills.

One of the most important aspects of anti-discriminatory practice is working with parents. While this aspect is covered in detail in Chapter 7, working with parents will be referred to here also.

Children come from families who are functioning within the wider context. This simply means that families are influenced by and influence others around them, including extended family, friends, work colleagues, religious and spiritual advisers and the network of health, care and education professionals in contact with families with young children. Individuals and families are influenced by the wider social culture within which they exist. The welfare and development of children within a family will be affected by the impact of these different influences on the family, even if they are not directly related to the child. For example, in a family where the mother speaks no English and is culturally isolated in a white British residential area, the children may miss out on pre-school experiences such as parent and toddler groups, playgroups and making friends in the neighbourhood. In other families, different expectations of boys and girls may influence children's choice of play and areas of development from a very early age.

Some things have no immediate 'cure'. Caring for a child with disabilities in a supportive environment, where his uniqueness is valued and his self-esteem is promoted, will not stop him experiencing discriminatory remarks, attitudes and behaviour outside the setting. However, it may help him develop resources to cope with hostility and prejudice from others and to ignore the negative evaluations of others. Encouraging children to play across the whole range of toys and activities in the early years setting will not ensure that they are not expected to play in a gender-limited way at home. Helping children who have already started to develop prejudices to re-think their approach to others can be very valuable in working towards the long-term goal of reducing discrimination in the wider society. No one worker can eradicate discrimination, but you may be surprised by how much can be achieved by working towards good practice in this area.

Cultural Diversity

Multiculturalism in Early Years Settings

Living and working in a multicultural society like Britain places specific responsibilities on early years workers in terms of the children and families they have contact with.

Article 2 of the CRC (UN Convention on the Rights of the Child, 1989) requires that the rights of all children be protected and promoted. It clearly prohibits discrimination against children based on their or their parents' or legal guardians' actual or perceived 'race, colour, sex, language, religion, political or other opinion, national, ethnic or social origin, property, disability, birth or other status'.

(Chalmers and Aggleton, 2003: 151).

Yet many children growing up in a wider culture dominated by white people may find few representations of their own family and community life in that context. Children (as discussed in Chapter 3) become aware of ethnic differences, in particular, at an early age. For many children entering the wider world, there is not only a lack of representation of their own culture, but also lack of knowledge and understanding of their cultural norms and beliefs, or hostility towards them. In practice, studies show that children of minority cultures often do not get the same level of attention and responses from early years workers as other children do (Ogilvy *et al*. 1990; Verhallen *et al*. 1989; Derman-Sparks, 1993).

Culture means the sorts of customs and practices, beliefs and ideas of a particular group of people. There are many important factors that determine differences between cultures, but the emphasis seems to continue to be placed on external factors such as dress, food and religious festivals. In many early years establishments, multiculturalism is translated into celebrating different festivals and wearing or displaying traditional clothing from a range of cultures. This type of multiculturalism can be a good way of introducing the idea of different cultures with different customs and practices to children, but there are limitations to this approach. A culture is not just a collection of costumes and eating habits, but is based on many subtle and less obvious factors, which cannot easily be summarized. Children learn about their own culture from birth and according to Millam (2002: 56): 'Cognitive skills and behaviour patterns, and the development of personality, are related to the cultural context in which children are brought up.' Culture, therefore, influences not only external behaviour but also how we think and feel.

Derman-Sparks (1989) warns us that by exploring other cultures only to remark on the differences in habits, festivals and clothing (the 'tourist approach'), merely makes other cultures seem exotic, while underlining their difference.

Children 'visit' non-white cultures and then 'go home' to the daily classroom,
which reflects only the dominant culture. The focus on holidays, although it
provides drama and delight for both children and adults, gives the impression
that that is all 'other' people – usually people of colour – do. What it fails to
communicate is real understanding.

(Derman-Sparks 1989: 7)

In some settings there may be only token efforts to tackle issues relating to a multicultural society, such as posters and displays. These are positive steps in themselves, but not helpful if they are confined to a limited range of articles and images.

The other issue that may cause confusion about the multicultural curriculum in early years settings is the fact that non-white cultures are often represented in stereotypical forms. Many people in Britain of Asian or African Caribbean heritage have adopted some of the dominant white cultural habits and beliefs. For example, many young Asian women in Britain do not wear traditional clothing in their everyday lives. On the other hand they may continue to follow other customs and beliefs relevant to their religion and culture. Cultural stereotypes are increasingly rare as all cultures borrow from each other and individuals, families and communities develop new cultural customs and habits over time. The use of traditional practices and customs may vary a great deal between individuals and families. For example, clothing, language and habits can all vary between individuals within the family and between families. We must be careful to recognize cultural diversity within ethnic groups as well as between ethnic groups. Pugh (2001) sums this up by arguing that the multicultural curriculum does not focus, for example, on British Indians or British Chinese but on Indians and Chinese, giving a false impression of how different cultural groups live in British society.

One of the problems may be that some early years workers may have only superficial knowledge and understanding of the range of cultures currently represented in Britain.

The key to working with colleagues, children and families in a multicultural society is to avoid both stereotypes and assumptions about individuals based on their external characteristics. We cannot assume that all people who appear to come from a particular ethnic group will behave in the same way. Culture is not a static concept, but one that changes over time.

(Think) **A Chance to Think**

Reviewing the ways in which we represent the range of cultures in Britain today can be helpful in determining if the early years setting is supporting individual children to develop positive images of their own culture.

Exercise 1

Within your placement or workplace, gather information about the activities that take place which focus on cultural diversity and answer the following questions:

1 To what extent are the activities ongoing and part of the every day experience of the children?
2 To what extent do they focus on diversity or more rigid stereotypes of minority cultures?
3 To what extent are parents and children involved in planning activities and giving advice about customs, beliefs and habits?
4 How is emphasis placed on the difference between cultures?
5 To what extent are the staff skilled and knowledgeable in this area?

Discuss your conclusions with a colleague or supervisor.

Learning about Diversity

In order to be able to support children in developing and maintaining positive images of their own culture, early years workers need to be knowledgeable about the range of religions, cultures and ethnic groups in Britain as a whole and in their local area in specific. 'Being knowledgeable' means understanding and respecting religions and cultures other than our own and recognizing the meaning of habits and customs relating to spiritual matters. Becoming knowledgeable takes time. The majority of early years workers will have absorbed quite a lot of information about other religions and cultures on their initial qualification course. If you are currently a student, you will probably have had some input on your course on multicultural issues. However, developing good practice and becoming a reflective practitioner involves building on basic knowledge and understanding and applying this knowledge and understanding in the workplace (this theme is covered in Chapter 9). So how can we find out more about other religions and cultures?

• talking to parents and children in a sensitive way about their lives
• reading about culture and religion in books
• reading relevant articles in reputable newspapers
• talking to colleagues and friends who come from different cultural backgrounds to yourself
• finding out about the range of different cultural activities in your own area
• maintaining an open mind and a deep respect for the values and beliefs of others.

Staff development may be available from the workplace or in the workplace, on issues relating to equal opportunities, anti-discriminatory practice and cultural diversity. If staff development is not available, you may wish to discuss with your supervisor how this might be introduced. Discussing any relevant issues in staff meetings or early years workers forums may help through sharing knowledge and ideas about promoting diversity on a daily basis.

Promoting Diversity

It is important that activities to promote religious and cultural diversity are not presented in the early years settings as an 'add-on' activity – something outside the normal range of day-to-day events within the setting. Too often multi-culturalism is trotted out at major festivals and then put away in between. In order to help children respect and value all cultures, acknowledgement of cultural diversity should underpin all activities. For example, cooking should cover the widest range of types of foods and preparation styles, bearing in mind food restrictions within some cultures and religions. Parents can be a mine of information about different recipes and ways of preparing food. Pugh (2001) reminds us that we need to avoid stereotypes in this area – it should not always be the Asian parents cooking the curry with the children and the English adult cooking the fairy cakes. As one young British Punjabi mother said, she was asked at nursery what her child liked to eat, and replied 'fish fingers'. The nursery nurse persisted and finally the mother realized that she wanted to know what sort of 'ethnic food' they ate in the family. The mother pointed out that her child did not much like curry, and that the answer was still 'fish fingers'.

Artwork and crafts can be a very creative area for promoting different cultures and customs. There are some excellent books depicting the artwork of different countries and cultures, which can be used to plan activities with children. Different uses of design and colour can be very exciting to a child who has produced many neat houses with rainbows behind them. Children can be encouraged to make collages which represent a broad view of the world, such as faces, animals, fruits, clothes and countries. Children can also model in clay, plasticine and papier mâché using different images as inspiration. As with all children's activities, it is the process not the product from which the child learns and develops.

Using images from a range of countries and cultures can be used as a basis for introducing new language to the child. For example, a successful activity involved looking at pictures of killims from Turkey. The rich colours and range of designs were very attractive to the children. While drawing killims using the same range of colours and planning simple designs, the adults and children talked about the carpets and how they were made and the country they came from.

Music is an important medium for children. The majority of children love to sing and dance. Traditional songs are commonly sung with children, but it is important to ensure that a wide range of traditions is considered within this.

Children may enjoy all types of music and they should be introduced to a wide range. Millam (2002: 170) suggests 'ballet, jazz, tap, modern, country and western, classical, reggae, soul, rap, calypso, garage and pop music, to name but a few'.

 A Chance to Think

There is no doubt that looking for new ideas takes time and effort. The rewards can be worth it, however, as the children enjoy new experiences and different types of stimulation. As your own knowledge base builds up and resources are gathered, the amount of effort may lessen.

 Exercise 2

Consider the following ways of finding new inspiration for day-to-day activities, which are based on the whole range of cultural diversity within British society:

- Visit libraries for reference books on art, different countries and cultures.
- Visit bookshops for the same and ask your manager if there is anything left in the resources budget.
- Ask parents if they have any music they are prepared to lend you or if they can share songs with you and the children.
- Ask parents and colleagues for ideas and resources to share.
- Read new and different storybooks to get ideas for themes, imaginative play and possibly displays.

Devise a new activity to do with the children you work with on placement or at work, which promotes cultural diversity in a non-stereotypical way. It could be making a display, a theme, art or craftwork or a game, song or story. Try to think of new sources of ideas to add to the list above. Share your work with a colleague or friend.

Language is a central influence on the development of children's sense of identity, their self-esteem and their knowledge and understanding of their own culture. Bilingual children are often seen as having a problem coping with two languages, instead of being valued and praised for their ability to communicate in two languages and to translate between them (Malik, 1998). In relation to the minority ethnic families she studied, Brooker (2002: 36) states that:

The ability to read and write in Bengali, and often in Arabic and English too, and to understand Hindi, does not confer social status, or grant access to the field of education.

It is important that the development of all languages a child communicates in are supported by early years workers, through images of the written language, bilingual books and story tapes, and adults willing to learn and use some words in other languages than their first. Labelling in a range of languages and introducing songs and poems in a range of languages are other methods of supporting children whose first language is not English and stimulating the learning of children who are monolingual. Non-verbal languages should not be forgotten. In one school, Makaton symbols were displayed around the classroom and used to label different objects to support the learning of a non-verbal child. The symbols also helped other children in the class to develop their use of Makaton to communicate with this child, and to learn another language.

Resources

Finding appropriate resources can be difficult and frustrating at times. We have all seen the black dolls which look like white dolls, the books in which families are portrayed as non-white but who behave like white families do, the videos which represent individuals from a range of cultures who all speak, think and act like white North Americans. However, resources that honestly and effectively represent a range of cultures can be found and built up over time. When considering new purchases the following should be considered:

- black dolls which have appropriate features but which are not 'dressed up' in traditional or ceremonial costume
- posters and pictures that draw on world art and represent different cultural images
- musical instruments from a culturally diverse range of sources
- cooking utensils for the home corner which reflect the diversity many children find in their homes, whatever their cultural background
- books which represent images of cultural diversity in a representative and honest way, including bilingual books
- music tapes or CDs of world music and the music which parents and children listen to at home
- food to cook which may be new to some children, but familiar to others – try different fruits and vegetables to eat, draw, dissect and discuss, different types of bread and staples (rice, potatoes, couscous, pasta), spices and herbs to smell, look at, draw and discuss and, maybe, cook with
- multipurpose dressing-up materials such as big scarves or long lengths of brilliantly coloured or glittery material that can be used to dress for a range of roles.

Asking parents and other staff for ideas is useful as a way of developing resources, as is visiting other early years settings where good practice is established.

Dealing with Racism

Promoting positive views of and responses to all ethnic and religious groups and individuals is part of the role that early years workers should take to develop anti-discriminatory practice in early years settings. However, the multicultural curriculum needs to be supported by clear policies for dealing with any form of racism in early years settings. Race is a concept used to describe groups of individuals on the basis of external characteristics, usually skin colour. In fact, all people come from the same race, and concepts of race are based on perceptions of differences that are superficial, rather than reflecting any real differences between individuals and groups. Although the concept of race is outmoded, the term 'racism' is used to describe discrimination on the basis of ethnicity or perceptions, often stereotypical, of an individual's culture, religion or country of origin.

Teaching children about diversity may contribute to the reduction in racism, but children are influenced by many factors outside the early years setting and the multicultural curriculum may not prevent racist behaviour. Allport (1954), cited in Tassoni and Beith (1999), defined several stages of behaviour arising from prejudice. In an early years setting racist behaviour could be:

- verbal abuse and name-calling
- avoidance: refusal to have contact with a child on the basis of race
- discrimination: exclusion from play and group activities
- attacks on children on the basis of race
- ongoing harassment of a child or group of children.

It may seem hard to believe that young children would behave in this way, but in many cases they are simply copying behaviour they have learned outside the early years settings. Verbal abuse and name-calling are generally the most common form of racist behaviour.

For many young white children there may be a lack of positive images of non-white people to offset the racist behaviour and attitudes they may learn from adults, the media and their observations of the position of non-white people in our society. Children become aware at an early age that some groups are valued more than others in some societies.

Dealing with racist behaviour effectively means working to create policy and practice which reflects a clear idea of the damage racism can have on the development of young children. One area that is sometimes disputed is whether general bullying policies are adequate to deal with racist behaviour. It is important to remember when considering this point that children who are subject to racism in the early years setting may also suffer racism outside the setting. Establishing a policy statement that is made clear to all parents and children is the basis of establishing anti-discriminatory practice. Policies, however, are statements of intent. In many ways the process of producing the policy has as much value as the policy itself, because this process helps to clarify how racist behaviour and attitudes will be perceived and dealt with. It can be an important learning experience for early years workers.

Children's behaviour should be monitored and any serious incidents recorded. Any form of racist behaviour should be responded to immediately. Young children may not know that their behaviour is offensive and possibly harmful to the other child, especially if they have seen adults behaving in similar ways. The behaviour should be stopped immediately and an adult should explain to the child or children involved why their behaviour is not acceptable. Any incorrect or misleading views expressed by a child should be firmly corrected (Tassoni, 1998). The child who has been on the receiving end of racist behaviour should be comforted and reassured. If children persist in repeating racist behaviour, parents must be involved. It is important to remember that more progress in changing behaviour may be made if explanations rather than accusations are used to respond to a child who has been racist. However, this should not imply a 'weak' response. The child must be left in no doubt that this behaviour is not acceptable and should not be repeated.

It is also important to ensure that all the children involved are aware of the negative impact and unacceptability of racist remarks or behaviour. Explanations and discussion of the issues are an important part of the process. For example, Gavin, 6, called a friend 'Paki' in the playground. He was sent to the head's office and reprimanded quite strongly for his behaviour. That evening at home, Gavin was quite upset and eventually explained to his mother that another friend, Mark, used this term regularly and that he had copied it without knowing what it meant. After discussion between Gavin's mother and school, the class teacher used circle time to discuss and explain the issues and to clarify acceptable and unacceptable behaviour for all the children in the class.

Sadly, racist behaviour in early years settings is not confined to children. Adults also behave in racist ways that may be harmful or hurtful to young children. It can be very difficult to tackle any incidents alone in an institutional setting. If you witness racist behaviour by another worker, it is important to record the incident and discuss it as soon as possible with the person in charge. You may feel able to discuss incidents directly with colleagues, but this should not be done in front of the children. As discussed in Chapter 3, the racist behaviour and attitudes of others can be harmful to the growth and development of young children. As Pugh (2001: 101) comments:

Grugeon and Woods' (1990) ethnographic study of primary schools identified a number of the effects of racism upon the self-images of South Asian children. Children were seen colouring themselves pink, describing themselves as having blue eyes and fair hair, they refused to go out in the sun in case they became brown(er), and avoided participation in minority ethnic festivals.

Gender Issues in Early Years Settings

Gender Divisions in Play and Behaviour

In a discussion about children's play activities, an example of a boy who wore nail varnish to nursery, had his hair done up in 'bobbles', like his sisters, and who regularly played with dolls was given. One student commented that the parents 'had to be brave' to allow this type of behaviour in public. There was a general sigh of relief when it was revealed that going into the wider world of the reception class had drastically reduced this behaviour in the child, as he absorbed the unspoken rules about gender-divided play from those around him. Despite the efforts of early years workers, we live in a society where boys and girls continue to develop different types of play, based on perceived gender differences. For example, anyone who watches the children's toy adverts on television in the weeks before Christmas is left in little doubt about the perceived appropriateness of different toys for girls and boys.

Studies show that children do play with different toys, according to gender. But gender in itself is a social construct, in the sense that how males and females behave and the social roles they take are determined by the society they live in. In different cultures, male and female gender roles can be quite different to those in modern western societies. Despite efforts to minimize the inequalities between males and females, through legal measures (see Chapter 3) policy and procedures, boys and girls are still subject to different expectations from those around them. Millam (2002: 12) cites a study by Miller (1987) in which psychology students sorted a wide range of toys into 'suitable for boys', 'suitable for girls' and 'suitable for both' on highly stereotypical lines. They also associated the 'boys' toys' with 'sociability, symbolic play, constructiveness, competition, aggressiveness and handling'. The 'girls' toys' were associated with the development of 'creativity, nurturance, attractiveness and manipulative skills'. Other studies show that children as young as 2 are choosing gender stereotypical toys to play with.

The stereotypes on which gender-divided play is based reflect stereotypes of male and female roles and behaviour within a society. By limiting children in their play, we are giving strong messages to them about the sorts of acceptable behaviour and occupations a boy or a girl should take part in, both as children, and as they grow up. This process becomes part of the child's socialization, perpetuating gender stereotypes in the next generation. Children may have their learning, their life experience, their aspirations and achievements limited by gender role expectations, which may make them feel that certain areas of knowledge, experience and behaviour are 'out of bounds'.

Anti-Discriminatory Practice and Gender

The first step in addressing gender issues in early years settings is to try to review our own attitudes and behaviour. Gender stereotypes are so firmly rooted in our social customs and expectations that we have to be careful not to assume that we are entirely free of them. In addition, if we believe that children should have choice and freedom to play as they please, it may be hard to dispute the gender-biased play seen in many early years settings. The very fact that the majority of early years workers in pre-school settings are female gives the children strong messages about who is responsible for nurturing and caring in society, as opposed to other social roles.

However, there are ways of promoting a wider play basis for girls and boys without dictating to them how they should play and what they should play with.

Perhaps one of the main ways in which early years workers can start to promote anti-discriminatory practice around gender in their setting is to ensure that resources are presented in a way that promotes non-gender-biased use. For example, if the home corner seems to be dominated by girls and avoided by boys, it may be necessary to make changes and to present a different type of home corner. In one situation, the home corner was turned into a police station after a nursery was visited by a police officer who talked to the children about what the police did. As a 'police station', the home corner was much more frequently visited by boys.

Think — A Chance to Think

Encouraging children to play more across traditional gender roles can be a slow process. Children can be encouraged to participate in non-stereotypical activities, but they may still choose to continue to play as they did previously. This may be because they are reflecting patterns of play learned elsewhere or because they are modelling the play of other children. In some cases, parents may actively encourage children to develop play in specific ways, based on their views of the appropriate behaviour of boys and girls. However, progress can be made, if early years workers are committed to change in this area. Children's imaginative play is full of the themes and roles the children see around them, reflecting social and cultural norms, according to Bruner (1972). So, even if the role-play is imaginary, children will adopt roles that are part of their 'real' life within it. Early years workers can present children with non-stereotypical images of adult roles to form a basis of play, through books and stories, themes and activities, and through gently challenging assumptions which are expressed by children and their families.

1 Go back and look at the observations you did on gender and play for Exercise 2 in Chapter 3 or complete this exercise now. Depending on what you have observed, make a list of suggestions for widening the restricted play to include both girls and boys, without pressurizing them to play differently.

2 Ask yourself if doing these observations has made you more aware of gender stereotypes in play and your own views on this. Discuss your conclusions with a colleague or supervisor.

Working with parents in this area is vitally important. There is evidence that parents have the strongest influence on children's understanding of gender roles and the development of gender stereotypes. Research shows that fathers are more rigid in their interpretation of gendered behaviour than mothers, particularly in respect of boys' behaviour. Parents need to be encouraged to discuss their ideas and concerns with you and to share views about play and gender.

Another issue to consider is the use of outdoor space by boys and girls. Boys have a tendency to dominate playgrounds with football and more vigorous physical play. It is important to consider how outdoor space is used for all the children and how both girls and boys can be encouraged to join in different types of games and activities. Boys may also enjoy different types of books to girls and therefore a range of fiction and non-fiction needs to be available to meet different tastes.

Here are some ideas which may encourage non-gender-biased behaviour in children:

- promoting themes which include males and females in non-stereotypical roles (men cooking, women truck drivers, male nurses and female doctors) built on reading, stories, role-play and artwork
- sensitively supporting single gender play to include both boys and girls
- changing areas of play in the setting which are consistently dominated by girls or boys
- creating an environment in which negative remarks about others are always considered unacceptable and gently but firmly challenged
- auditing and getting rid of resources which reflect gender stereotyping, such as books, story tapes, games and toys
- ensuring the setting has many images of men and women in nurturing roles and women and men in a range of job roles
- being a role model yourself in terms of non-stereotypical behaviour and roles
- challenging colleagues and parents who unconsciously or consciously present children with stereotypes of males and females.

Anti-discriminatory practice around gender issues is not confined to encouraging children to avoid stereotypical behaviour. Early years workers also have a responsibility to ensure that the early years environment is free of assumptions about children on the basis of gender. Studies show that carers of young children can reinforce different behaviours in boys and girls through different expectations. Boys are generally expected to be more active, aggressive, competitive and outgoing. Girls are generally expected to be quieter, more nurturing to others, compliant and well behaved. Sometimes the things adults say to children reinforce these stereotypes. For example:

- 'Be a big boy' – don't show emotion
- 'Be a good girl' – do as you are told
- 'He's just a boy' – supporting competitive or aggressive behaviour
- 'She's a tomboy' – she'll grow out of this unruly behaviour.

Think · A Chance to Think

Language can be very important in conveying subtle meanings to children. The type of language we use in terms of gender should be carefully considered in order to ensure that gender stereotypes are not being reinforced. For example, if we always refer to the child's carer as 'mum' we reinforce the view that it is always females who look after children. For example, 'You'll have to ask your mum' or 'Your mum will like that piece of work'. Sometimes it is quite hard to detect the assumptions that are hidden in language, such as referring to certain job roles as 'he' (doctors, lawyers, fire-fighters and police officers). These stereotypes are reinforced in many images that children are familiar with such as Bob the Builder, Fireman Sam, Barbies and dressing-up clothes sold with 'for girls' and 'for boys' on the boxes. Early years workers need to challenge these familiar stereotypes through their own use of language and avoidance of stereotypes.

Exercise 4

Spend a few days making notes within your work setting or placement on how gender stereotypes are reinforced through language. In many settings, examples will be rare because of effective anti-discriminatory policies and practices. Look for examples of good practice, where gender stereotypes are challenged appropriately and children are encouraged to think and behave in non-stereotypical ways. Make a record and share it with a colleague or supervisor. Remember to be tactful and not embarrass any of your colleagues with direct criticisms.

Anti-Discriminatory Practice and Disability in Early Years Settings

Supporting Children with Disabilities

One of the most positive steps for children with disabilities is to be cared for and educated with other children where possible, rather than segregated into special provision. For some children whose needs are great and who require the maximum amount of support, integration may not be possible, but for the majority of children with disabilities, learning and developing in a group situation is perfectly possible with the right support. Perhaps the most important factor in anti-discriminatory practice with children with disabilities in early years settings is to ensure that they are seen as children first and foremost and not described in terms of their impairment. For example, Owen aged 4 came home from nursery and talked at length about a new child in nursery who he had taken a liking to. At the end of the description, which involved how nice the other boy, Allan, was and how he played and what he looked like, Owen said 'Of course: Allan's blind – that means he can't see – and sometimes I help him with little things, but only if he wants me to.' The nursery had clearly introduced the new child sensitively and thoughtfully, so that his blindness was seen as just one, perhaps not very significant factor about him. In addition, the other children supported Allan, but only when he asked for help, leaving him in control.

Hobart and Frankel (1999) state that up to 20 per cent of children are estimated to have disabilities including:

- physical impairment
- sensory impairment
- learning difficulties
- medical conditions
- need for special diets
- behavioural and emotional difficulties
- a combination of any of the above.

Describing children in terms of their disability negates them as people and limits our vision of their potential progress and development. Children should not be described as 'the blind boy' or 'the girl with learning difficulties' as this is demeaning to them and labels that child in a negative way. Similarly, there are many terms for describing children with disabilities, many of which are denigrating. Children should be discouraged from using these and staff should ensure that they provide good role-models in the language they use. Some children may have learned words such as 'mongol' or 'spastic' outside the early years setting. Many adults still use inappropriate terms to describe people with disabilities, without perhaps understanding how these may be distressing to that person. In a conversation with her tutor, one student described how she had been focusing on one child in the private day nursery she was on placement in:

Student: She's a . . . I don't know what to call her . . . you don't call them 'mongols' any more, but she's like that . . . she's got learning difficulties, that's it . . . or it's something syndrome.

Tutor: What's her name?

Student: Mary.

Tutor: Perhaps you could call her Mary.

At the other extreme, adults may try to over-protect children with disabilities or treat them as if they were much younger than their years. This may feel like positive action to safeguard the children, but it can prevent the children from developing higher levels of independence and may stultify their ability to make progress with their achievements. Finding a balance can be difficult and may involve working hard at communicating with the child and the parent.

Parents may vary in their attitudes – some may encourage the child to be as independent as possible, others may worry about how the child is coping, or be over-protective. It is important to work with the parents and to listen to their fears and concerns and to try to reassure them. Parents of children with disabilities may have already had a difficult time, coping with a child with additional needs and possibly with siblings as well, and in many cases struggling to get appropriate support and help. It is important not to judge if parents see the early years placement primarily in terms of respite for themselves. Early years workers may be an important source of information for parents of children with disabilities. Communication should always be open and honest and early years workers should respect parents as partners in the decision-making process about any child with disabilities needs (Wolfendale and Wooster, 1996).

Early years workers should not be anxious if there are details of a child's impairment which they are unaware of. There is a multitude of different types of impairment and early years workers will not have knowledge and understanding of all of them. However, it is important to ensure that relevant workers find out any information about the child's needs or any possible risks to the child, through asking the child and the parent, relevant reading or staff development and training. Gaining general knowledge about a particular impairment should not influence the way in which the child is seen as an individual.

Another problem that often arises for children who have disabilities is the 'Does he take sugar?' syndrome, which manifests itself as an assumption that anyone with a visible disability cannot either understand or speak for himself. Anyone who has spent time in a wheelchair, however temporarily, will have probably noticed that all communications are addressed to the person pushing it (and probably found how frustrating and annoying this is too).

Some children do have communication difficulties and these need to be dealt with appropriately. Children should be encouraged to talk directly to children with disabilities even if there may be no answer, and not to talk about a child with disability as if she is a piece of furniture. For example, in one infant school, a child was learning to communicate through signing in Makaton. Makaton signs were displayed all over the school and other children learned the basic signs in order to communicate with him. This seems a very positive way of enhancing the communication skills of all the children within the school. In addition, the child was allocated a 'circle of friends' in Reception class who were responsible for supporting him in his everyday life, for example, going to the cloakroom, lunchtime, play time. By KS2, these friends had become very capable young people through taking on this responsibility and developing caring and communication skills.

Finally, children with disabilities need to participate fully in the activities and play within the early years settings. This may involve adult support and some consideration of types of activities to ensure they are not planned in a way that makes it impossible for some children to access them. Careful consideration of the indoor and outdoor environment is needed to ensure that it is accessible to all children and that children with disabilities can maximize their independence within the environment. Toys and activities should be accessible to all children and consideration should be given to specialist toys which can be used more easily by some children. If parts of the environment need to be changed to accommodate the needs of a particular child, this should be presented in a positive light for all children, not as a nuisance.

Disability Awareness in Early Years Settings

Helping other children and sometimes parents to accept policies of inclusiveness and integration for children with disabilities is part of the development of anti-discriminatory practice. Children who have had little contact with people with disabilities may be curious and inquisitive about a child with a visible disability or see the child as different (Malik 1998). It is important not to reprimand children for this interest, but to channel enquiries into more acceptable modes through role-modelling appropriate behaviour and explaining how certain ways of expressing questions may be hurtful to the other child.

Resources should reflect positive images of children with disabilities. Stories are particularly helpful, because they can be used to present everyday images of children with both visible and non-visible disabilities. They can also reinforce images of children with disabilities which do not show them as either victims or targets for abuse, and which do not emphasize any impairment as the most important thing about the child. Early years workers who are not confident about good practice in this area should seek staff development or training which emphasizes disability awareness and an integrated approach. Children should learn about positive attitudes to people with disabilities even if there are no children with impairments in the setting. This involves introducing positive images of people with disabilites, answering questions honestly and avoiding presenting children with disabilities as victims to be pitied. It is also important to get away from standard stereotypes of children with disabilities, such as images of bravely smiling children in wheelchairs, and to remember that there are many types of impairment that may affect children's ability to learn and develop.

Creating a Safe and Supportive Environment for All Children

There are many other groups and individual children who may suffer discrimination on the basis of perceived differences. Children can be ostracized for being poorly dressed, for being a child 'looked after' by the local authority, for wearing glasses, being small or other physical features, or because they are being raised in households with lesbian or gay parents. For example, a study (Thomas and Beckford, 1999) on the outcomes of adoption found that although children felt that they gained from being adopted, they did not want their adoptive status known at school for fear of being bullied. Although certain types of discrimination are common enough to require particular attention, it is important not to forget that many other children are subject to discrimination for a wide range of reasons.

Creating a supportive environment for all children involves initially developing a common attitude within the staff team, which is positive, child-centred and reflects clear views on respect for all, shared decision-making and shared responsibility. This type of environment involves adults respecting children and not just expecting respect, and encouraging children to be involved in developing the early years environment. Themes, stories and topics which address important issues about how we behave towards others and a climate which promotes praise rather than criticism are important stages in developing the environment. The contributions of parents are crucial within this (see Chapter 8), as is the belief that parents know their children best. David (1993) suggests 'whole school development' to create an environment in which all children could feel safe and valued. This could include:

- implementing an effective policy on bullying
- working with parents, children and all staff to develop mutual trust and respect
- creating time and space to listen to children
- building opportunities for praise and support into everyday activities

- promoting themes and topics about care of self and others
- developing assertiveness and confidence in young children through themes and topics
- involving all members of the early years setting in decision-making
- emphasizing respect and mutual care between children and children, adults and adults and children and adults.

Creating a positive environment can help children learn that all individuals are different and special and that there are many different ways of approaching everyday activities (Tassoni, 1998).

Developing a positive environment for young children to learn and develop in will not happen overnight. It is a dynamic process that involves consideration and implementation of measures to make changes happen. Quality in early childhood care and education is discussed in detail in Chapter 5.

Think A Chance to Think

Listening to children is probably the main key to understanding their real experience both within the early years setting and outside. In most settings, whether they are home-based or institutional, which involve one worker or more, it is often difficult in a busy day to identify time for listening to children. However, in order to understand the meaning of the child's experience to herself, this time needs to be found.

Exercise 5

Over a period of a few days, note down the opportunities within the day's routines and activities which children could use to communicate thoughts and feelings to adults and in which adults could listen to children. Make some suggestions for further promoting opportunities for adults and children to communicate in this way. Share your answers with a colleague or supervisor and check the sample answer in the Appendix.

Conclusions

In this chapter, some of the ways in which equality of opportunity can be promoted within early years settings through anti-discriminatory practice have been discussed. The multicultural curriculum has been analysed in terms of the possible negative outcomes of cultural 'tourism' and the need to discuss the range of different cultures in terms of real every day lives rather than just stereotypes of traditional behaviour. Anti-discriminatory practice has been presented as an ongoing development of positive work practices and policies, which reflect the needs of particular groups of children who may suffer discrimination. The value of developing a safe environment for all children in which every individual is valued and respected has been examined, as has the need to work with parents to achieve this. Finally, the need to listen to children and to make time to do this has been discussed, in order to ensure that children's thoughts and feelings and real experiences form the basis of planning anti-discriminatory practices.

REFERENCES AND FURTHER READING

Bruner, J. S. (1972) *The Relevance of Education*. London: Allen and Unwin.

Chalmers, H. and Aggleton, P. 'Promoting Childrens' Health Through Nursing Care', in J. Brannan and P. Moss (eds) (2003) *Rethinking Children's Care*. Buckingham: OU Press.

David, T. (ed.) (1993) *Educating our Youngest Children: European Perspectives*. London: Paul Chapman.

Derman-Sparks, D. (1989) *Anti-Bias Curriculum*. Washington, DC: National Association for the Education of Young Children.

Derman-Sparks, D. (1993) 'Challenging bias in child care', *Coordinate*, **33**, 8–13.

Hobart, C. and Frankel, J. (1999) *Childminding: A Guide to Good Practice*. Cheltenham: Stanley Thornes.

Malik, H. (1998) *A Practical Guide to Equal Opportunities*. Cheltenham: Stanley Thornes.

Millam, R. (2002) *Anti-Discriminatory Practice: A Guide for Workers in Childcare and Education* (2nd edn). London: Continuum.

Miller, C. L. (1987) 'Qualitative differences among gender stereotyped toys: implications for cognitive and social development in girls and boys', *Sex Roles*, **16**, 173–487.

Ogilvy, C. M., Boath, Z. H., Cheyne, W. M., Johada, G. and Schaffer, H. R. (1990) 'Staff attitudes and perceptions in multicultural nursery schools', *Early Childhood Development and Care*, **64**, 1–13.

Pugh, G. (ed.) (2001) *Contemporary Issues in the Early Years: Working Collaboratively for Children* (3rd edn). London: Paul Chapman, in association with the National Children's Bureau.

Tassoni, P. (1998) *Child Care and Education*. Oxford: Heinemann.

Tassoni, P. and Beith, K. (1999) *Nursery Nursing: A Guide to Work in Early Years*. Oxford: Heinemann.

Taylor, J. and Woods, M. (eds) (1998) *Early Childhood Studies: An Holistic Introduction*. London: Arnold.

Thomas, C. and Beckford, V., with Munch, M. and Lowe, N. (1999) *Adopted Children Speaking*. London: British Association of Adoption and Fostering (BAAF).

Verhallen, M., Appel, R. and, Schoonen, R. (1989) 'Language functions in early childhood education: the cognitive linguistic experiences of bilingual and monlingual children', *Language and Education*, **3**(2), 109–30.

Wolfendale, S. and Wooster, J. (1996) *Meeting Special Needs in the Early Years*. London; David Fulton.

5

Quality in Early Years Learning and Development

INTRODUCTION

Early childhood is considered to be a distinct phase of development, within which children's learning and development are more intense than at any other stage of life. Froebel (1782–1852) saw this phase as crucial, and he believed that children should be carefully nurtured during the early years to promote their learning and development (Froebel, 1887). It is during this phase that children develop the foundations of their skills, knowledge and understanding for later in life. The types of experiences children have during early childhood are crucial in terms of their learning and development. The support young children receive at this stage is important, as is the way in which young children are encouraged to learn, the activities they are presented with and the opportunities they have for first-hand experiences and exploratory play.

Children do not learn and develop in a vacuum. Their experiences are determined by a whole range of different influences, including the family system, parents' social and work patterns, friends and community, children's care and education experiences and the wider culture and environment within which the child and family lives. Bronfenbrenner's (1989) ecological approach summarizes these influences as a series of concentric circles depicting the interlinked influences on a child's learning and development (Bee 2000).

Early years workers have specific responsibilities within this phase. The care and education of young children involves understanding children's developmental needs, being able to assess a child's stage of development and respond with appropriate support and monitoring and recording progress. Early years workers need to understand how children learn and how learning can be supported through a range of measures including structured activities and child-led play. Education is not just the formal processes children go through in nursery classes and school, but all their experiences at home and in the widest range of care and education settings. Education is also not just about children's cognitive development, but their social, emotional, physical and language development too.

In this chapter, we shall explore some of the different views of early years education and the inextricable connections between the care and education of young children, embodied in the concept of 'educare'. The arguments for high quality early years care and education will be discussed, as will methods of achieving good standards in this area. The type of curriculum and the skills and abilities required by early years workers will also be explored. Differing views of ways of achieving high-quality educare for young children will be discussed, taking into account holistic views of children's needs and how they can be met.

Exploring Quality in Childcare and Education

Views on the Purposes of Early Years Education

Different early childhood theorists have discussed the process of and purposes of child education in different ways. For some educational theorists, the main purpose of education for young children is to help them to learn the requirements of the society and culture within which they live, while developing their own potential to the maximum (Mellor, 1970; Vygotsky, 1978). Education not only prepares children to become fully part of their own culture and society, but also supports children in developing their own skills, ability, knowledge and understanding. In addition, child education should support children in learning the skills of learning, which can be used throughout their lives. In Vygotsky's view, others, such as adults, are very important in helping to transmit cultural beliefs, norms and practices to children. He also believed that children's cognitive development took place within interactions with others, making the social context of learning central to child education.

McMillan (1930) believed that educational services should support the development of the whole child, including their health and general well-being. She supported the view that education of young children should help them build confidence in themselves and considerations for others. Like Froebel, she recognized that young children should be carefully nurtured in the early years. Piaget placed much less emphasis on the social context of learning and development. He believed that children needed to learn at their own pace, developing mental schemas within which they assimilated experiences gained from interaction with the external environment. Children deal with new experiences by the process of accommodation, by which they extend and modify their schemas in response to new information. Education, in Piaget's view, is largely undertaken by young children themselves, as they experiment with their environment and gain new understandings from it.

The purpose of education for young children can be seen diversely, but perhaps summarized as:

- a recognition of the importance of the early years as a stage of development
- an acknowledgement that young children need an appropriate environment in which to learn and develop
- the need to ensure that adult involvement is supportive, sensitive and enabling rather than prescriptive
- the belief that young children have their own learning goals and the ability to pursue these with the appropriate environment and support
- the holistic nature of child learning and development
- the value of social development, emotional stability and language development in supporting cognitive development.

Understanding educational theory is important in developing a view on why we educate young children and the importance of the style of, and approach to, the child's learning experiences. Developing quality in early years care and education is dependent on this understanding.

Education and Care

Ideas about the education of young children cannot be separated from views on how they should be cared for. The Rumbold Report (Department of Education and Science (DES), 1990) summarized a growing belief among those working in the field of early childhood care and education, supported by research, that the care and education of children could not be viewed separately. This divide had long been a source of concerns for those involved in early childhood care and education. Much of this separation was historical, based on the development of young children's educational provision through local authority education departments and the development of care services through social services departments and the private and voluntary sectors. Children's developmental needs are viewed more holistically now, rather than compartmentalized into health, care and education needs, and in response to this multidisciplinary or integrated services are being developed, such as the early years or young children's services discussed in Chapter 2. The term 'educare' refers to both the philosophy of integrated service provision and the provision itself.

The development of educare has had a significant impact on concepts of quality in children's learning and development, such as:

- increased emphasis on the development of the 'whole child'
- closer cooperation between different early years professionals
- recognition of the wider influences on a child's learning and development
- commitment to closer working partnerships with parents
- integration of services in some areas.

Projects such as Sure Start have pioneered new ways of working with children and families to provide services in more coordinated ways. Children and families can access health, education, care and advice services, among others, through Sure Start projects established to meet the needs of children up to 4 years and their families in the most disadvantaged neighbourhoods. The development of children's centres in some areas also provides a single access point for a wide range of services required by families and children. While half-day nursery grant-funded early years education places are available for all 4- and (in 2004) all 3-year-olds, many providers are also offering full day care as well in order to meet the needs of working parents.

The Green Paper 'Every Child Matters' (DfES, 2003) lays out plans to extend the integration of services to children and families through full service schools providing education, health and social care services and through Sure Start Children's Centres in some areas. The planned integration of services within local authorities through the development of Children's Trusts, with a single Director of Children's Services responsible for education and children's social services, is aimed at bringing together children's services in a much more structured and universal way.

Developments in Quality in Early Years Services

There has been a growing emphasis on issues relating to quality in early years services in recent years. The Rumbold Report (DES, 1990) reflected some of the issues involved in improving quality as described above.

The Children Act 1989 set out a philosophy of interaction with children and their families that emphasized partnership with parents and between service providers and which promoted child-centred approaches.

Defining quality in early years services is not entirely straightforward. Not all concepts of quality are agreed on by early years professionals. Brophy and Statham (1994) draw on one of the volumes of guidance accompanying the Children Act ('Family Support, Day Care and Educational Provision for Young Children', 1991) to look at the 'main factors which influence quality of care'. These include three different ways in which quality can be envisaged:

1 **Child development** – good quality 'educare' should enhance the child's development.
2 **Rights and expectations** – good quality 'educare' should be based on the concept of fulfilling children's rights, which will cover all aspects relating to their development.
3 **Value-based** – assessing quality requires making value-judgements, therefore it should be clear what the criteria for making these judgements are.

In evaluating a study of measuring quality in playgroups, Brophy and Statham (1994) came to four important conclusions to contribute to discussions on quality. They are:

- Definitions of quality are essentially value-based.
- Definitions of quality change over time and therefore measures of quality must also develop over time: developing quality is a dynamic process.

- Quality can be viewed from the perspectives of the children, the parents and the early years workers at least, therefore the quality of services can be partly assessed by the extent of development of the partnership approach.
- Equal opportunities policies and practices are central to quality both in terms of the range and type of services and individual services.

Quality measures must have a clear value-base and should reflect both general and specific areas of work with children. Quality measures need to develop over time and be flexible to ensure they measure relevant aspects of educare. Woods (1998, p. 203) states that 'quality is a value-laden and dynamic term, often meaning quite different things to different people even within the same organization'. As such, quality is hard to define in early childcare and education settings, because it does not 'stand still'.

More recently there has been a number of developments aimed at ensuring better standards in early years services. In response to concerns about lack of consistency in inspection standards across local authorities in the UK under previous legislation within the Children Act 1989, the Care Standards Act 2000 paved the way for registration and inspection of all daycare and childminding settings by OFSTED from September 2001. OFSTED created the Early Years Directorate to perform this function and the National Standards for Under Eight's Daycare and Childminding were published in 2001 to provide a national framework for registration and inspection of all daycare settings. The 14 standards cover:

1. A suitable person to care for children.
2. Organization of the setting.
3. Care, learning and play.
4. The physical environment.
5. Equipment.
6. Safety.
7. Health.
8. Food and drink.
9. Equal opportunities.
10. Special needs.
11. Behaviour management.
12. Working in partnership with parents.
13. Child protection.
14. Recording and documentation.

Curriculum Standards

The introduction of the Curriculum Guidance for the Foundation Stage (QCA, 2000) established a standard curriculum for 3–5-year-olds within a defined stage of learning. The Education Act 2002 was extended to make the six areas of learning within the Foundation Stage a statutory curriculum. Children in nursery grant-funded places and reception classes now work towards Early Learning Goals through a curriculum designed for the early years as described within the Guidance. The Foundation Stage curriculum is based on individual development through a series of stepping stones towards reaching the Early Learning Goals. These stepping stones are achieved through a structured, play-based curriculum outlined in the Guidance. There are six areas of learning, each with related Early Learning Goals. They are:

- Personal, social and emotional development.
- Communication, language and literature.
- Mathematical development.
- Knowledge and understanding of the world.
- Physical development.
- Creative development.

The introduction of the Foundation Stage provided a National Curriculum for 3–5-year-olds in nursery grant-funded places for the first time. One of the main changes affected reception classes, which became part of the Foundation Stage. Many establishments have created a Foundation Stage Unit comprising reception and nursery classes. Reception classes now have to offer a play-based curriculum linked to nursery education, rather than focus on preparation for KS1. In some schools this may have required a change in both perception of the role of reception classes, the content of the curriculum and the style of teaching and learning. Reception teachers, whether part of a dedicated unit or not, have to plan and coordinate the curriculum with nursery staff. However, despite this, reception classes are expected to introduce the National Literacy and Numeracy Strategies as dedicated 'hours' by the end of the year.

In 2002/3 the Foundation Stage Profile replaced baseline assessment as 'a single national assessment system for the Foundation Stage' (www.qca.org.uk). The Profile has to be completed by the end of the child's year in reception class, but it is expected that the summary profile will be drawn from ongoing assessment of the child's progress towards the Early Learning Goals within the six areas of learning throughout the Foundation Stage. There are no tests or set assessments in order to complete the Profile. Best practice guidance suggests that Profiles are completed as part of ongoing observational assessment of children. Profiles are used to inform parents and Year 1 teachers of the child's progress and attainments at the end of the Foundation Stage.

The development of a good practice framework for settings working with 0–3-year-olds resulted in the document 'Birth to Three Matters' (www.surestart.org.uk), outlining four aspects of the child's care and development which should be focused on within the setting. These are:

- A strong child.
- A skilful communicator.

- A competent learner.
- A healthy child.

Each aspect has four components for the setting to focus on in their work with the child.

A Chance to Think

There is a range of views on the factors influencing quality in educare for young children. Within the Foundation Stage, the Early Learning Goals dominate as a requirement, as does the National Curriculum in schools. Some views of the factors determining quality go beyond these fairly limited, subject-specific goals and emphasize not just the content of learning, but also the context. For all children, pre-school and school age, providing quality should be linked to, but not limited by, the official curriculum.

Exercise 1

Before reading on, write down, from your own experience and knowledge, the factors you think are most important in the provision of quality educare to promote the learning and development of young children. Include anything that you feel is relevant. Share your comments with colleagues and ask if they can add to your list.

Benefits of Quality Care and Education to Children

It is important to summarize why quality has become a central issue in studies and debates about early childhood and to determine the benefits of a quality agenda. Although we cannot define quality in educare in any global way, the concept currently implies working towards higher standards in meeting children's holistic needs and promoting 'whole child development' through better integrated services and partnership between early years workers, parents and children. The benefits of high quality educare for children impact on the children, parents and the wider society.

The benefits to children of high quality educare can be summarized as follows:

- promoting all aspects of the child's development, within the context of her family and the wider society and culture
- acknowledging the child as an individual in terms of his unique self, his stage of development and his individual needs

- developing the child's social sense, knowledge and understanding of the socio-cultural context in which she lives and the values held within the wider culture
- ensuring equality of opportunity for all children to develop their potential and achieve within the full range of their abilities
- supporting children's rights as members of society and potential citizens:

The benefits to parents may include:

- providing opportunities to work and study
- enhancing and extending the care and education they provide for their child within the family
- forming partnerships with early years workers to develop an integrated approach to meeting their child's needs
- using support systems and role-models to enhance their parenting approach.

More general benefits to society as a whole might include:

- socializing of children into the wider culture
- establishing social and moral values in the coming generations of adults
- developing the potential of future citizens to a higher standard in order to meet the social, political and economic requirements of society
- possibly reducing expenditure on dealing with the social costs of juvenile crime and delinquency and support schemes for children in trouble (health, education, social services).

High quality educare in the early years is seen as a vital preparation for children to take their place in society as adults and to learn the skills to do so effectively. In an increasingly complex, industrial society in which technological change is driving social and cultural change at a rapid rate, the gap between those who grasp the opportunities within this and those who cannot has the potential to become extensive. The debate about high quality educare is closely linked to the wider debate on social exclusion and inclusion, which is currently significant within the social and political agenda in the UK. This debate has been extended recently by proposals to further integrate children's services to improve quality made in the Green Paper 'Every Child Matters' (DfES, 2003), as discussed in the section 'Policy and the Rights of Young Children' in Chapter 2.

Working to Achieve Quality in Early Years Care and Education

There are a number of factors that contribute to quality in children's learning and development, which can be summarized from the discussion above, and which have direct relevance to the development of good practice among early years workers in a range of roles and settings. These include:

- knowledge and understanding of children's developmental needs and methods of meeting them
- an holistic approach to childcare and education
- the content of the curriculum and how it is delivered
- the resources and environment available
- monitoring and evaluating of children's progress
- working with parents and other professionals
- equality of opportunity
- staff development and training.

Because some of these factors have been covered more fully in other chapters of this book, we shall focus on the first five points.

Knowledge and Understanding of Children's Developmental Needs

In order to meet a child's individual needs, it is important first to know what they are. Early years workers learn about the different aspects of child development and the theoretical basis for these, but we need to look at good practice in applying this knowledge. Young children vary in their stages of development, often to a great extent where specific learning or developmental delays are evident. Age is a guideline, but should be used with some caution. In learning about a child in a specific stage of development the early years worker should find out as much about the child from the parents as possible. The child may have developmental needs, which are not obvious initially. Information about any developmental delays or problems should not be used to label children, but to understand them better. For example, a child may have a sensory disability, or be in foster care which may have involved a move from the original carers and the breaking of attachments. Information about the individual child must be kept confidential (see Chapter 8).

Good practice in meeting the social and emotional needs of children involves ensuring that the child is made to feel safe and secure within the setting. Children need to be accepted for their individuality and made to feel that they are warmly regarded by the early years worker. Children entering the setting for the first time should be made to feel welcome, helped to find their way around, and shown the toilet, the resources and where to hang their coats. Early years workers should listen to children, giving them attention and letting them know that the things they have to say are valuable. Children should not be shouted at, spoken to coldly or dismissively or made to feel that they are a nuisance. Adults act as role models for children and should ensure that they behave in ways that they would expect the children to behave. Respect for each other is an important principle in early years settings and should apply to all relationships within that setting.

Children's physical needs should be met with regard to the child's sense of dignity and integrity. Children should be encouraged to do as much as possible for themselves within their capabilities, including putting clothes on and taking them off, as soon as the child is capable of doing so. Children should not be left to struggle if they are having difficulty achieving a task. Sometimes children may ask for help when they have previously coped alone. The child may be seeking closeness, feeling tired or needing extra support that day, and this should be taken into account. Young children should be encouraged to develop choices in food and drink, and to feed themselves where possible. They should be given opportunities for physical activity including dance, play and games.

Comments about children's physical ability, size and body shape should be discouraged. Recent studies have shown girls as young as 7 are body conscious and worried about being fat. Children should never have their self-esteem damaged by being compared with others or made to feel clumsy or incompetent.

 A Chance to Think

Developing an environment where there is respect between individuals depends largely on the behaviour and attitude of the adults within that environment. Respectful relationships can be built on listening, genuine interest in the child and his thoughts, feelings and activities, firm boundaries and controls and warmth.

Exercise 2

Read the case study and answer the questions below. Compare your answers to the sample answers in the the Appendix.

JAS

Jas is starting at private day nursery next week. She is 22 months old and has a hearing impairment. Jas has not had many social contacts because her parents have worried about how she will cope. The health visitor talked to them about Jas going to nursery or playgroup because she was not developing socially and seemed afraid of other children. She is an only child. Jas and her mother, Suki, are coming to nursery tomorrow to discuss Jas's needs. The family are Muslims living in a predominantly white area.

1 Describe the needs you think Jas may have. Try not to focus entirely on the consequences of her hearing impairment.
2 How might you try to meet these needs within the nursery?

3 Is there any other information you might need about Jas and her family?
4 What sort of help might you need and how might you get it?

An Holistic Approach to Childcare and Education

In 1999 there was a series of articles in the *Guardian* about secondary schools and how they met the needs of children. One article focused on a school that was catering for a whole range of pupils' needs, many of which would be described as social, emotional, cultural or personal. Many of the pupils came from difficult home backgrounds, in which some of their basic needs did not seem to be getting met and where the children experienced stressful relationships and events. The article reminded readers of the simple truth that children cannot benefit from learning if the rest of their needs are not being met.

The proposals of the Green Paper 'Every Child Matters' (DfES, 2003) reflect this theme – that children's needs must be addressed holistically through integrated services, reflecting all areas of the child's development, not compartmentalizing needs and ignoring the influence of unmet need in one area on progress and achievement in another. One of the proposals, to develop 'full service extended schools', suggests that in the future a much wider range of services to children will be delivered through schools. Breakfast clubs, out-of-school activities, homework clubs, health services and family support services may all be delivered through school on a much more widespread basis than currently exists.

This is not to say that teachers and other school staff must learn to deliver health and social care services themselves! However, it does mean that schools may become much more closely involved with the range of their pupil's needs and their families. Early years staff will be expected to develop closer relationships with a wider range of other professionals, a theme that will be discussed in more detail in Chapter 7.

As educationalists or childcarers, early years workers need to focus on the whole child and not on one aspect of the child's development. Theorists such as Vygotsky (1978) emphasized the social nature of cognitive development as described above. Bruner's (1972) ideas about the social nature of learning are based on the notion that children essentially develop cognitive skills through their social interactions. Not only are social interactions crucial to cognitive development, but also the type of cognitive skills developed are culturally determined.

Looking at the child as a whole means acknowledging that children will not be able to benefit from the play and activities if other needs are not being met. For example, if a child has problems with her social development, this may impact on her ability to participate in and enjoy play. Smilansky (1968) believed that socio-dramatic play is important for the development of social, cognitive and language skills in children. She developed a scheme of play tutoring which helped small groups of children to develop skills in socio-dramatic play through adult involvement. The study showed that the children played more spontaneously in this way after the play tutoring. This approach was considered to be especially useful for children from less advantaged backgrounds who showed little spontaneous socio-dramatic play. The study has been criticized because it is possible that the developmental progress shown by the children was due to spending more time with an adult, rather than because the children were involved in more socio-dramatic play. However, it seems to support the view that in order to learn through play, children's other developmental needs also have to be met.

 A Chance to Think

Meeting the whole range of a child's needs involves knowing what those needs are, as discussed above, but also knowing how emotional and social issues can affect a child's ability to learn and develop. For example, the syndrome of 'failure to thrive' in babies and young children is known to be connected to emotional neglect as much as to physical neglect. Children who have suffered abuse or neglect, or many changes of caregiver, often have cognitive developmental delays and do less well at school.

 Exercise 3

Read the case study and answer the questions below. Compare your answers to the sample answers in the Appendix.

EDDIE

Eddie is 3 and has just started at nursery. Eddie lives with foster carers who have cared for him for two months. Before coming to live with his current foster family, Eddie lived with another foster family for over a year and before that with his mother. He came into care because of physical abuse and neglect. He had to leave his previous foster family because they decided to stop fostering for personal reasons. Eddie has language development delays and is quite withdrawn. He likes to watch TV but does not play much. He is a quiet child who does not always respond to adults. Eddie is small and thin for his age and the foster carer is concerned that he does not eat well. Eddie has not lived in this community before.

1 What do you think are Eddie's immediate needs at nursery?
2 How could these needs be met?
3 What problems might Eddie have in adjusting to nursery?

The Content of the Curriculum and How it is Delivered

The curricula for young children currently reflect a renewed confidence in the role of play in learning and development. The Foundation Stage curriculum is designed to be delivered mainly through a combination of structured play activities and children's self-chosen play, supported by adults. As discussed above, this has renewed play-based learning in some reception classes where preparation for KS1 had limited play as a context and tool for learning. However, there are still differences in views on the respective values of adult-initiated and child-directed play activities. Is children's self-directed play a useful tool for learning and development? Or should play be adult-directed to ensure learning takes place in accordance with the demands of the curriculum? The role of play in learning and development has long been the subject of debate in the field, with a range of theoretical positions to consider.

For example, Hutt's (1979) model of play demonstrates her belief that children do not develop cognitively through free-flow (ludic) play, but that they gain knowledge through exploration of new objects or features of the environment (epistemic play). Piaget's work on stages of play implied that children do not learn through play, but that they use play as a method of integrating or assimilating new experiences into their understanding. For example, a child may have the experience of going to the zoo. In order to add this experience to the structure of the child's understanding of the world (his schema), he may play at 'zoos', repeating the events at the zoo through role play on his own or socio-dramatic play with other children.

Vygotsky (1978) firmly believed that children demonstrated their highest levels of ability through play, and the 'pioneers' (Froebel, McMillan and Isaacs) all advocated play as the main medium for learning. Bruner (1972), however, had less time for free-flow play. He believed that children learned about expectations within their culture from games with rules.

So, does child-directed play have a role in the curriculum for young children? One of the problems of studying the role of child-directed activities in learning and development is that this type of play is essentially difficult to evaluate. In play children have the opportunity to explore their own learning needs and to practice new skills and ideas about their environment. Play is often social, developing both social and language skills and contributing to emotional development. Children can learn how to deal with conflict and other interpersonal interactions in the safety of a play situation.

Good practice in curriculum planning and delivery should ideally include time for both free-flow play and structured activities. Child-led play should be valued as much as adult-led activities. Bennett *et al.* (1997) argue that teachers theoretically support the role of play as a medium for learning, but in practice may be uncertain about how to incorporate this in the curriculum.

Adult intervention in play should be focused on supporting and extending the play to enhance the children's learning and development. Insensitive intervention can negate the play. Intervention should always be based on observation. Adults can intervene in play in a variety of ways:

- joining in child-led activities
- initiating activities
- supporting children to join group play
- helping children to extend play
- dealing with conflict.

Early years workers should be supportive and responsive to the themes in children's play, recognizing that children focus on their own learning needs through play.

Structured activities should always be planned so that children can have the maximum choice within them. It may look nice to send home a pre-prepared cut-out shape decorated with crinkled tissue paper from nursery, but did the child really benefit from just gluing the tissue paper on? The child may have benefited a lot more from choosing a shape to cut out or have cut out for her, then deciding the decorations from a wide range of natural and manufactured materials, even experimenting with different methods of attaching the decorations. It is important that children should be allowed to experiment and make mistakes and to use materials in their own way. The child who pours water over the paper or chops it into little pieces may not be conforming, but he may be finding out a lot about the properties of paper and water.

A Chance to Think

Structured play activities need to reflect children's learning needs, not just occupy their time and produce a 'product'. The curriculum often focuses on the whole group of children, but there may need to be variation in activities to meet differing needs.

Exercise 4

Think about the activities you planned and delivered with children one day recently. Write down how they contributed to the whole child's development (social, emotional, language, physical, cognitive). How did the activities support the children in their own culture? Did the children enjoy the activities? Did themes from the activities appear in the children's free-flow play? Think about your conclusions and decide if the activities could have been done differently to enhance the children's learning and development more.

Resources and Environment Available

Resources vary between settings, depending on budgets and space. Children should have direct access to resources if possible so that they do not need to ask for them. Space should be kept uncluttered for safety reasons and also because a cluttered space may inhibit play. On the other hand, avoid clearing away equipment which is in use for a non-conventional purpose. Good practice in this area involves balancing the quantity of bought toys and natural or found objects and multipurpose equipment such as scarves and shawls for dressing-up. Bought toys should always be looked at carefully. Are they fun? Can they be used in different ways and for different purposes? Do they look nice but have few functions? Can the children use them easily by themselves? Play areas usually have a range of toys and equipment including dolls, construction toys, small world, dressing-up, art materials and dough as basics. Consider the uses of the following:

- a box of shells
- some large dust-sheets
- sparkly shawls
- some large lightweight boxes
- a bag of leaves, twigs, moss and stones.

Traditional play equipment can be varied by the addition of found or natural objects, or materials as described above. One notable example of developing play materials for very young children was Goldschmied's 'treasure basket' (Goldschmied and Jackson, 1994).

The 'treasure basket' contained a range of household and natural objects which babies could explore with their hands and mouths. These included stones, hair curlers and other objects which had a range of colours and textures. Older babies were encouraged to experiment with the objects during quiet play periods, finding out about their properties (will this curler go through the middle of the other one?) and to use them in more interactive play with each other.

Monitoring and Assessing Children's Progress

Records of each child's progress and attainments should be kept in line with organizational requirements. Children at the Foundation Stage will have their achievements recorded in the Foundation Stage Profile. This may be an ongoing process or may be a summary assessment when the child reaches the end of her reception year, depending on the setting. This Profile is used to inform Year 1 teachers and parents of the child's progress and to identify any areas where the child may have significant delays or special needs. For example, one 4-year-old boy's dyslexia was first identified through observations of his difficulties with emergent writing in nursery. This information alerted his Year 1 teacher to observe his progress closely and action was taken to identify his dyslexia and provide support at an early age. This early identification of specific difficulties or special needs is a crucial outcome of monitoring and assessing children's progress and attainments. However, the possibility of special needs or learning difficulties should always be considered within the context of the very wide range of developmental progress different children make at any particular age.

At the Foundation Stage, assessment should be ongoing, through observations of the child in a range of situations and activities and at different times. This information should be fed into the child's Profile but should also inform you of the child's developmental needs; progress; play interests and themes; social development; emotional condition and level of contentment within the setting. Observations should be analysed to inform planning, including the need to differentiate activities to meet individual children's needs. They should also form the basis of informal and formal feedback to parents, or for raising concerns about any aspects of the child's learning and development with the parent.

Observations are not an end in themselves, but a tool for gathering information about a child. Analysing observations and drawing conclusions from them should be a crucial part of the planning cycle. Similarly, observing children merely to complete records of attainment and progress ignores the contribution of such observations to curriculum planning in line with identified need.

Children at KS1 will have their progress recorded within school and this will be assessed through SATs at the end of Year 2, when the children are about 7 years old.

Conclusions

Good practice in supporting child's learning and development is rooted in quality issues and in the way these are translated into practice. National policy currently focuses on more structured approaches to learning, based on achieving Early Learning Goals and the National Curriculum. However, in order to meet the needs of the whole child, a range of different activities needs to be provided, including child-led play and structured activities.

REFERENCES AND FURTHER READING

Bee, H. (2000) *The Developing Child* (9th edn). Needham Heights, MA: Allyn and Bacon.

Bennett, N., Wood, L. and Rogers, S. (1997) *Teaching through Play*. Buckingham: OU Press.

Bronfenbrenner, V. (1989) 'Ecological systems theory', *Annals of Child Development*, **6**, 187–249.

Brophy, J. and Statham, J. (1994) 'Measure for measure: values, quality and evaluation', in Moss and Pence (1994).

Bruner, J. S. (1972) *The Relevance of Education*. London: Allen and Unwin.

David, T. (1993) *Educating our Youngest Children: European Perspectives*. London: Paul Chapman.

Department of Education and Science (DES) (1990) *Starting with Quality: Report of the Committee of Inquiry into the Educational Experiences offered to Three and Four Year Olds* (Rumbold Report). London: HMSO.

DfES (2001) 'National Standards for Under Eight's Daycare and Childminding.'

DfES (2003) 'Every Child Matters.' (summary)

Department of Health (DoH) (1991) *The Children Act 1989 Guidance and Regulations, Volume 2: Family Support, Day Care and Educational Provision for Young Children*. London: HMSO.

Froebel, F. (1887) *The Education of Man*. New York: Appleton.

Goldschmied, E. and Jackson, S. (1994) *People under Three*. London: Routledge.

Hutt, C. (1979) 'Play in the under 5's: form, development and function', in J. G. Howells (ed.) *Modern Perspectives in the Psychiatry of Infancy*. New York: Brunner/Marcel.

McMillan, M. (1930) *The Nursery School*. London: Dent.

Mellor, C. (1970) *Education through Experience in the Infant Years*. Oxford: Blackwell.

Moss, P. and Pence, A. (eds) (1994) *Valuing Quality in Early Childhood Services: New Approaches to Defining Quality*. London: Paul Chapman.

Moyles, J. (1994) *The Excellence of Play*. Buckingham: OU Press.

Piaget, J. (1959) *The Language and Thought of the Child*. London: Routledge and Kegan Paul.

QCA (2000) 'Curriculum Guidance for the Foundation Stage.'

Smilansky, S. (1968) *The Effects of Socio-Dramatic Play on Disadvantaged Preschool Children*. New York: John Wiley.

Sure Start (2002) 'Birth to Three Matters.'

Taylor, J. and Woods, M. (eds) (1998) *Early Childhood Studies: An Holistic Introduction*. London: Arnold.

Vygotsky, L. (1978) *Mind in Society: The Development of Higher Level Psychological Processes*. Cambridge, MA: Harvard University Press.

Woods, M. (1998) 'Early childhood education in pre-school settings', in Taylor and Woods (1998).

Keeping Children Safe

INTRODUCTION

On first consideration, the issue of children's safety may seem to be fairly straightforward. All early years workers clearly have a responsibility to ensure that the children in their care are safeguarded from exposure to accident or infection. However, when we look into safety issues more closely it soon becomes clear that this principle of good practice is a minefield of different views and opinions, and that the concept of 'safety' applies to a much wider range of aspects of the child's health, well-being, growth and development.

For example, the parents of Dan (aged 8) believe that children should be allowed the maximum freedom possible to become mature, independent individuals. They allow Dan to go to the park across the road on his bike with his friends. However, the parents of Cherry (also aged 8) believe that 8-year-olds are not equipped to deal with some of the problems that may arise when out on their own. They are concerned about children 'falling-out', leaving one child isolated from the group, vulnerable to abduction or attack. They also feel that children of this age might not know how to deal with an accident. Cherry is not allowed to go to the park without adults and feels angry and 'left out' because of this.

There is no 'right' and 'wrong' in this case. Parents, early years workers and society as a whole are all concerned with the safety of children, but how this is interpreted in the case of individual children can be very variable. It is also important to remember that physical safety is only one aspect of the safety issue. Children also need challenges and stimulation to develop psychologically and emotionally, to mature and achieve. These needs may sometimes require a relatively more physically 'risky' environment in order to be fulfilled. For example, a shy 7-year-old gained a great deal of confidence from going rock climbing, because she was able to achieve at this activity. Her mother was terrified at the prospect of sending her child on what appeared to be a high-risk activity, but eventually agreed because she felt that the social and emotional benefits outweighed the physical risks.

Children can never be made be absolutely safe. Every part of living has some risks attached to it and efforts to eradicate all physical risks to the child could result in creating such a stifling environment that the child is in danger of suffering from complete lack of stimulation. One of the current debates in early years care is the way in which some children in western societies are denied the opportunity to play outside because of safety reasons. Increasingly, many children are transported by car between school and home, and to and from planned activities. Some studies have concluded that children are gradually losing access to a world of free play which is 'owned' and controlled by children, and in which older children develop responsibility through caring for younger children. Parents and carers are increasingly concerned about the dangers of traffic and child abductors or molesters. The increased sophistication of mass media communications means we have access to a much wider and more vivid range of information about child abduction cases. The outcome is, from one point of view, increased restrictions on children's freedom to mix freely and play in their own world. From another point of view, we live in an increasingly unsafe world and children need to be protected from potential and actual dangers within that world. Balancing the child's need for freedom, free play and the opportunity to develop coping skills in the wider world against the need to ensure children are safe and secure is no easy achievement.

However, early years workers looking after other people's children have a solemn responsibility to ensure that the children are cared for in a way that is safe and which provides the child with a feeling of safety. Reducing the risks in the environment to an accepted level is part of the role of the early years worker. Some of this is obvious – fires must have guards, electrical appliances must be kept out of children's reach, street doors must be kept locked, toxic substances must be kept away from children. But there are also areas of uncertainty. Should Shaun (3) be allowed to try to climb the large frame when there is a risk of falling? Should Dawn (4) be allowed to cut out with sharper scissors to get a neat edge? Is it safe for David (13 months) to practise walking outside when he already has a bruise on his forehead from falling over?

This chapter explores the dimensions of safety for children of different ages, the risks of both under-protection and over-protection and the balance between physical safety and children's rights to explore their environment, take risks and become more independent. The debates and concerns about child safety will also be looked at in the context of wider society and changes that have taken place over time in childcare practices. The early years workers' responsibility to protect children from abuse will be considered as well as good practice in terms of emergency procedures and record keeping in the context of legal and workplace requirements.

Legal Issues in Child Safety

There are a number of legal requirements that all providers of early years care and education need to comply with.

Health and Safety Act 1974

The Health and Safety Act 1974 makes it the responsibility of all employees to be aware of safety issues and to respond appropriately to them. This includes ensuring that any safety equipment provided is used; behaving in a way which maintains safety and does not endanger others; and reporting any potential safety hazards which may result in accidents or ill-health.

Employers are responsible for providing a safe environment and maintaining it appropriately. You should be aware of the main premises of the Act, which should be displayed in all settings. You should also be aware of safety procedures and policies within your workplace, including action to be taken in response to accidents and fire evacuation procedures. If you are not aware of these procedures, then it is important to take this up with your supervisor to ensure you and any colleagues are fully up to date with safety requirements in your workplace.

Schools are required to comply with Health and Safety guidelines from the LEA.

National Standards for Under Eights' Daycare and Childminding (DfES, 2001)

All daycare providers and childminders need to be able to demonstrate that they are providing a safe environment for children in order to meet the requirements of registration and inspection. Many of the 14 standards on which OFSTED registration and inspections are based deal with safety issues. These basic standards are criteria for determining the suitability of a setting or provider and failure to meet them may result in failure to become registered, or even de-registration.

The national standards which refer to safety are:

Suitable Person (1)

All settings must be in the charge of a suitable person. This should exclude individuals with criminal records with convictions that may affect their suitability to care for children, for example, those with offences against children, violent offenders, and drug offenders. The Protection of Children Act 1999 reinforced measures to ensure convicted offenders could not access jobs working with children. All early years practitioners and anyone else intending to work in a role which brings them into contact with children must now obtain a disclosure from the Criminal Records Bureau (CRB) before taking up their post.

Organization (2)

The setting should have a registered person who is accountable for standards including ensuring the adult:child ratio complies with specifications; training and qualification requirements are met; and appropriate use of space and resources are complied with.

Physical Environment (4)

Premises must be safe, secure and suitable for the purpose. There must be adequate space in an appropriate location, with access to necessary facilities for a range of activities.

Equipment (5)

All furnishings and equipment must be appropriate for the purpose they are used for, must conform to relevant safety standards and be well-maintained.

Safety (6)

The registered person must promote safety in the setting and on outings, and take precautions to prevent accidents.

Health (7)

The registered person must promote good health, take steps to prevent infection spreading and take appropriate measures when illness is identified.

Food and Drink (8)

Food and drink should be made available regularly, should be adequate for the children's needs, properly prepared and nutritious. It should meet dietary and religious requirements.

Equal Opportunities (9)

The equality of all children should be promoted through anti-discriminatory practice.

Behaviour (11)

Practitioners should be able to manage a wide range of behaviour in ways which promote the welfare and development of all children.

Child Protection (13)

Child protection procedures should be developed in all settings in line with Area Child Protection Committee procedures and all staff should be aware of them and comply with their requirements.

Documentation (14)

Records should be kept and policies and procedures developed to ensure the efficient and safe management of the provision.

It is important to remember, however, that these are minimum requirements, not maximum and that good practice may demand that providers go beyond these standards in some areas as discussed in the sections below.

Creating a Safe Environment

Whatever the context of care and the role of the early years worker, there is a duty to ensure that the physical environment is safe for the children being cared for. Obviously, there is an age dimension to this aspect of safety. Some of the precautions needed to ensure the safety of toddlers might be superfluous for the care of 5- and 6-year-olds. However, there are some basic safety guidelines which apply to the majority of early years settings and which should always be followed. The majority of accidents take place in the home, so it is important to remember that indoor environments contain many potential hazards for children.

Indoor Safety Guidelines

- Cover plug sockets with plastic guards and check flexes for fraying at regular intervals.
- Keep medicines away from children in childproof containers, discard unwanted medicines and ensure that all medicines are correctly and clearly labelled.
- All heating appliances should be child-safe using equipment such as fireguards.
- Windows should be locked and have catches fitted to ensure that they open only a few inches; children should not be allowed to open or close windows.
- Smoke alarms should be fitted; fire drills should be known to all staff and regularly practised.
- Street doors should be kept locked and have handles that children cannot reach; there should be notices to ensure all visitors close them on entry or exit.
- Safety gates should be used to protect younger children at the top and bottom of stairs.
- Cupboards, fridges and other kitchen appliances should be fitted with catches or locks as appropriate.
- Sharp objects should be kept in a safe place which is not accessible to children.
- Toxic substances (e.g. cleaning fluids, glue, alcohol, polish) should be kept away from children.
- Matches, lighters and any other fire-lighting equipment should be non-accessible to children.
- Equipment suitable for older children should not be made available for younger children, including toys and play materials.
- Regular clearing up and putting away of toys and equipment improves the safety of the environment and should include a check for damage or wear and tear which might lead to injury.
- Food must be stored at the correct temperature, hygiene routines must be followed when handling food and all stale and old food should be disposed of immediately.

- Keep the environment clean, especially kitchens and bathrooms, and dispose of all waste immediately and safely.
- Cooking facilities should be made safe and all cooking activities supervised at all times.
- Kettles, hot drinks and other sources of potential burns or scalds should be kept well away from the children.
- Irons should never be left unattended and should be switched off when not in use and put somewhere safe to cool.

Think) *A Chance to Think*

Indoor safety depends to some extent on the type of environment you are working in. If you are in your own home, it may be that you have to pay a lot more attention to safety issues than if you are in a purpose-built early years environment such as a nursery. Childminders also have the problem of ensuring that other adults and older children in the household are aware of safety issues and conform to agreed guidelines. However, the main and most important way of ensuring child safety is to be vigilant in terms of watching out for potential hazards and to ensure children are properly supervised according to their age and stage of development.

Exercise 1

1 Think about your work environment or placement. Look at the safety guidelines above and check whether they are being complied with. Can you add to the list? What other more specific guidelines apply to the particular age group of children you care for?
2 Check the safety guidelines supplied in or for your place of work. Are they all being complied with? Is there anything that might be usefully added to the guidelines? Discuss any concerns with your supervisor.
3 Check how parents are informed about safety in your workplace and how they can contribute to keeping children safe, for example by sending children in appropriate clothes and footwear, shutting doors and gates, not allowing children to wear jewellery or bring potentially hazardous materials into the early years setting.
4 How do you deal with safety issues as they arise in your workplace? How do you review your approach to safety, and are safety reviews done regularly?

Outdoor Safety Guidelines

- All equipment should be age-appropriate, placed in a safe place on a suitable surface and supervised.
- The outdoor environment should be safely contained with no access to the street.
- Toxic substances should not be used on grass or plants in the outdoor area and gardening equipment should be locked away at all times.
- Poisonous plants and trees should not be planted.
- Dogs should not be allowed access to the play area and any dog faeces should be removed immediately.
- Children should be dressed appropriately for the weather and sun-cream and hats used on sunny days, with special care for fair or freckly children.
- Children should wash their hands after playing outside.
- Ponds should be covered or fenced and children should never be allowed to play near water unsupervised.

Think *A Chance to Think*

Children need to have the space to play outside and explore the environment. Gardens and other green outside spaces are perfect in many ways for young children to start to find out about the natural and physical world. Children should be able to get dirty, to pick up worms and snails and look at mini-creatures in the grass and on plants. In summer, playing in a paddling pool or sprinkler can be really pleasurable, as can using outside equipment such as swings, slides and climbing frames. Outside spaces give children the chance to build physical skills and confidence, such as trike and bike riding, ball games and climbing.

Exercise 2

1. Look at the paragraph above and think of the benefits of outdoor play for children of different ages. What are the potential hazards of the activities mentioned? How could these be minimized? Look at the sample answers in the Appendix.
2. Look at the outdoor play area at your place of work or placement. Are safety guidelines being followed? What other safety issues are relevant in your particular workplace and for the age group of children you work with?
3. How could the outdoor environment be made more interesting for children without increasing the risks to child safety?

Planning for Safety

The most important factor in ensuring safety for the children in your care is planning. Planning should include the ways in which the environment is organized, the ages of the children and the ways in which children access the environment and objects within it. Planning should also include how to respond to an accident or other safety issue and how to review policy and procedures. All individuals involved in the early years environment should be involved in planning for safety and should be aware of safety issues and procedures and know what to do in an emergency. This should include the children on an age-appropriate basis. Planning must be in accordance with any relevant policies and legislation (relevant legislation will be looked at later in the chapter.)

Accidents happen because of lack of foresight and thinking ahead to anticipate potential hazards. Tragic cases reported in the media include a child who died when he fell on to a sharp knife sticking up in the dishwasher, a child who stepped on faulty Christmas tree wiring and was electrocuted and a baby who drowned in the bath as his mother spoke on the phone for a few minutes. Cases like these can contribute to a sense of panic about children's safety and the feeling that it is impossible to protect children from danger. However, the majority of hazards can be avoided by forward planning, good routines and clear guidelines to adults and children about how to behave in different situations.

Plans should include the following:

- Records on the children should include any conditions which put the child at risk (such as if a child has a food allergy) and these should be known to all staff and other adults in the setting.
- Emergency and first aid procedures should be known to all staff and other adults in the setting, including contact numbers and procedures if there is an accident.
- Evacuation procedures should be known to all and practised with the children.
- Deployment and storage of equipment, materials and other objects in the environment should not impede exits and should not increase risk; heating appliances should not be blocked, fire exits must always be clear.
- All safety procedures including those for evacuating children should be revised in response to the needs of the particular children in the setting, thus if a child with visual impairment joins the setting, safety guidelines should be reviewed in the light of her specific needs.
- Clear instructions should be given and put up in writing in respect of fire procedures, including the location and use of different types of fire extinguishers.
- Disposal of waste should be planned so that there are no potentially toxic substances where children may have access.

The purpose of planning is to ensure that problems are anticipated and dealt with before they arise. However, although child safety is of vital importance, the child's needs to be stimulated and to gradually learn how to deal with potential dangers as he matures and grows must also be met. An environment that is safe, but unexciting, will not do! Many activities, which might initially appear hazardous, can be completed successfully with careful planning. For example, cooking with children involves a number of potential safety issues, but if children are properly prepared and given clear guidelines and good levels of supervision, then cooking can be a fun, safe activity that contributes to a wide range of the child's developmental needs.

101

Exercise 3

Imagine you are setting up either an indoor or outdoor play area for a specific age group of children. Make plans for ensuring child safety in this environment, including reference to the following issues:

- layout of the space to be used
- equipment and toys
- access
- levels of supervision required
- potential hazards
- dealing with emergencies
- guidelines for adults and children
- ensuring the environment is stimulating and varied.

You may like to draw a plan of your environment to show how you would arrange it. Share your work with a colleague or supervisor and ask them for additional ideas.

Next, plan an activity with a small group of children in a specific age range, for example an outing, an experiment, a new game. List the potential safety hazards and how they could be avoided or dealt with. Check that the activity is stimulating and enjoyable for the children, as well as safe.

Safety Equipment

All early years environments should have basic safety equipment. This can include highchairs for young children to sit in for meals and drinks, safety gates to prevent babies and young children falling on the stairs, fireguards and cooker guards. Some of the other safety equipment available is listed above. It may seem enough of a precaution to ensure that such equipment is available. However, as with so many things, it is how the equipment is used which constitutes safe practice, not the equipment itself.

In considering the use of safety equipment the following guidelines may be useful:

- Regularly check the condition of any safety equipment used and replace or restore any damaged equipment immediately; test smoke alarms at regular intervals and replace batteries.
- Always carefully check the condition of any second-hand equipment before buying, making sure that there is no damage or wear and tear which may affect the functioning of the equipment.
- Make sure that everyone who uses safety equipment knows how to use it properly, for example fireguards which fasten to the wall.
- Regularly check that equipment is being used properly.
- Store equipment in a safe place.
- Keep any safety equipment clean.
- Report any damage to safety equipment to the appropriate person in group settings.
- Ensure that all staff know how to use any specialist equipment for specific children properly, such as wheelchairs.

(Think) *A Chance to Think*

The use of safety equipment is a routine which early years workers are involved in all the time. It is easy sometimes to forget the purpose of these routines and in some cases, to get into habits of not using equipment properly. For example, how many times do we see young children travelling in buggies without the straps fastened? Worse still, how often do we see young children in the back of cars with unfastened seatbelts? Safety arrangements need to be reviewed at regular intervals to ensure that they are effective and relevant to the children's needs and ages.

Exercise 4

Using your workplace or placement as an example, complete a safety equipment audit by answering the following questions.

1 List the safety equipment in use, including all equipment used directly with the child and other equipment used to keep and make the environment safe, such as smoke alarms and fire extinguishers.
2 Check that all the equipment is in good working order and not showing signs of damage or excessive wear and tear.

3 Do you know how to use all the equipment properly? If not, find out!
4 Do all other staff or adults on the premises know how to use the equipment properly?
5 Find out the arrangements for checking safety equipment, reporting any problems, replacing any obsolete or damaged equipment and training staff to use equipment in group settings.
6 Find out about any guidelines or policies on the safe use of equipment in your setting.

Safety Routines

Perhaps the most important safety routine for all early years workers is the everyday supervision of children's activities. Levels of supervision need to be related to both the age and ability of the children involved. The key to appropriate levels of supervision lies in knowing the children well. Some 4-year-olds can be relied on to use outside equipment safely and sensibly, combining caution and adventurousness in a way that makes the play both enjoyable and safe. Other 4-year-olds can be entirely reckless at times and need much higher levels of supervision to be able to play safely. Realistic expectations of children both in terms of their age group and individual character and ability are central to good standards of supervision. Babies and young children need high levels of supervision in all their activities, as they have no understanding of potential hazards in their environment.

Another essential routine is the fire drill, which should be regularly practised in all settings so that it is familiar to both children and adults. All staff and volunteers should be well versed in evacuation procedures in the event of a fire or other event. Childminders should have an escape plan and should practise this with the children so that they are familiar with the process. Other adults in the house should know the escape plan and how they should contribute to evacuating the children in the event of a fire.

Routines should also include the regular inspection of rooms, equipment, electrical and gas appliances, windows, doors, outside play areas and equipment and safety equipment to ensure they are functioning appropriately and do not present any sort of danger or hazard.

There should also be specific safety routines for certain activities with children, which should be known to all workers in the setting. For example, cooking with children should always include the following safety precautions:

• Choose cooking activities according to the age and ability of the children.
• Supervise the use of all equipment and ensure that children use sharp knives and other potentially dangerous tools only under supervision when they are old enough to do so safely.

- Use cooker guards and keep children away from hot ovens.
- Always lift hot food containers yourself.
- Make sure children wash their hands before cooking and do not eat part-prepared food such as cake mix with raw egg in it.
- Turn pan handles away from the edge of the cooker.
- Cook with small groups so supervision levels are high.
- Do not leave children in kitchen areas without adult supervision.

Other activities should have similar safety routines and these should be known to all staff and any helpers or volunteers.

Safety routines about collecting children should be developed and strictly applied in all settings. Children should be collected only by designated adults and all staff should be aware of who can pick up a particular child. If there is a particular cause for concern, for example, an adult who has been excluded from contact with a child by the courts, extra vigilance is needed. If in doubt, it may be necessary to keep the child until a designated person has been contacted. Parents should be made aware of your policy as regards collection of children and should be strongly discouraged from sending different people to collect the child. One after-school club operated the following policy:

- a locked door which was opened only by a staff member
- a check on every adult who came in to collect children to ensure they were designated adults
- each child was signed out as they left.

This policy ensured that no children 'disappeared' either on their own or with an inappropriate adult, during the scramble to collect children between 5 and 6 p.m.

Similar policies should be developed to ensure that visitors do not have unsupervised access to the children and cannot wander around the setting at will. If you are in doubt about the policies or procedures about collecting children and supervising visitors in your workplace or placement, check with your supervisor.

Taking Children Out

One of the most enjoyable activities early years practitioners can do with young children is to take them out of the setting and do something completely different for a period of time. The children benefit from the break in routine, the different type of stimulation and experiences they may have during an outing and the new thoughts, ideas and first-hand knowledge they bring back to the setting to use in their activities. Some early years workers, such as childminders, take children out regularly as part of their daily routine. Trips and outings can be stimulating for workers as well, providing them with a change of pace and a new perception of the children and how they behave in different environments.

The problem with trips is that they immediately present the early years workers with a whole new range of safety issues to consider. These can appear daunting at times, perhaps resulting in ideas for outings being abandoned because they are too complex to arrange safely. However, not all outings have to be elaborate. One little boy of 3 walked to the local pet shop with two nursery nurses and a small group of children, to buy a tank for goldfish. Another group went later to fetch the fish and food. The boy talked about this short, simple outing for weeks after, describing the pet shop and the animals and equipment that could be bought in it. He drew the tank and fish several times, displaying his sense of pride and ownership gained from being involved in buying them for his class.

The key to successful outings is careful planning, well in advance. Each trip will have unique features, which need to be considered, but there are some general areas which should be planned for:

- The child/adult ratio should be suitable to the ages and numbers of children.
- Extra adults need to be available for children with special needs who require extra support.
- Children should be well prepared for the outing, within their age and understanding, so they know what is expected of them on the trip.
- Parents should be advised about footwear, clothing and any other requirements well in advance of the trip and staff should check that all essential items have been packed e.g. medication, sun-cream, contact numbers, first aid kit.
- Parental permission must be given in writing.
- Transport should be planned for safety, including issues such as insurance, safety belts, eligibility of drivers and condition of the vehicles to be used.
- Systems for 'tracking' all the children should be agreed beforehand so all adults know which children they have charge of.
- Avoid crowded destinations where it may be difficult to keep track of the children.
- Adult helpers or volunteers should have clear instructions and preferably be part of the planning process.
- Emergency arrangements should be made, especially if children are of the age where they may wander off. Staff should have a list of children.
- Contingency plans should be made, including contact names and numbers if there is a problem such as a child becoming ill on a trip.
- Any permissions from managers and insurance requirements should all be complied with well before the trip takes place.

If you have not planned an outing before, the responsibility may seem over-whelming when all the possible pitfalls are taken into consideration. However, as with so many aspects of safety, the main issues can be dealt with by forward planning and some careful consideration of the potential risks of the outing.

Exercise 5

Plan an outing for the children you care for in your workplace or placement. Write out your safety plan, taking into account all aspects of the outing, including what to do in emergencies and who to contact if there is a problem. Describe the discussions you need to have with parents, other staff and the children before you go on the trip. Discuss your plan with a colleague or supervisor and ask if they can add to it.

Childminders and other home carers such as nannies may take smaller numbers of children out much more regularly than other early years workers. Although the same considerations apply for outings further afield, there are some specific guidelines for regular everyday trips to the park or shop.

- Put babies and small children in buggies or prams, ensuring they are properly strapped in and appropriately dressed for the weather.
- Cross roads at designated crossings, hold hands and remind toddlers and young children of road safety rules. If a child is unreliable on the road and you have several children to care for, you may consider a harness if parents agree.
- Always put brakes on prams and buggies when you stop and do not leave children outside shops or other buildings in a pram or buggy.
- Supervise children closely in the park and avoid areas where dog faeces are common.
- Discuss expectations of behaviour on trips with children, according to their age and understanding.
- If you are going out in the car, ensure children have their own seat and safety belt, be very careful of traffic when getting several children in and out of the car, be sure the car is in good working order and your insurance covers outings with children in your care.
- Do not take children out if they are ill, unless it is absolutely essential to do so.

Teaching Children to Be Safe

Part of the role of an early years worker is to help children to understand and absorb safety rules according to their age and ability. We cannot do all the thinking, planning and taking of precautions for children until they are 16 and then suddenly turn them loose on the world! Children need to know about safety and how to be safe, and to gradually internalize safety instructions so they become automatic in the older child.

Babies

Babies should be firmly discouraged from exploring plug sockets and other electrical sources, sharp objects, cupboards, fridges and cookers and all other potential safety hazards. A firm 'no' while removing the object or the child from the danger zone is the first step in helping children to understand and avoid danger. Very young children will not understand why they are being limited in their behaviour and cannot be expected to understand the concept of danger, but firm instructions should still be given to begin to establish a pattern of safe behaviour.

Toddlers and Pre-School Children

Toddlers are into everything and have to be supervised very closely in order to curb their capacity for seeking and finding danger. Adults need to continue to give firm instructions while removing the child from the danger or the danger from the child. Young children may go through phases where they seek adult attention by approaching potential hazards or behaving in an unsafe way. In these cases it is important to deal with the situation with the minimum of fuss, merely removing the child from the situation and reminding the child of the danger in a calm voice.

As pre-school children grow older they begin to understand the concept of danger and to internalize safety instructions. This does not mean that adults should stop reminding the child of safe behaviour, but that the child should be praised for remembering safety rules and guidelines and carrying them out. For example, remembering to carry scissors with their points down, walking carefully while carrying objects, looking for cars while crossing with an adult, washing hands before meals or after handling substances such as glue or paint, pointing out breakages or spills to an adult. Children of this age are beginning to understand and respond to various potential hazards, but are generally not reliable. There are also wide differences between children of the same age that should be taken into account.

Children of this age can be given simple instructions about 'stranger danger', such as explaining that they must not go off with any other person who asks them, even if they have seen that person before. It is helpful to remind children about this aspect of safety at intervals and to remind them whom they can go with at the end of their time with you. Although you will have systems in place to ensure that children are collected only by designated adults, part of a child's growth to independence includes starting to internalize safe behaviour. It is useful to discuss 'what would you do if?' scenarios with children to check their understanding of this aspect of safety. However, it is important not to alarm children and make them fearful by over-emphasizing the dangers.

School-Age Children

As children leave the very early years behind and become more reliable and responsible, they are able to more fully internalize safety rules and apply these with fewer reminders. As children enter this phase, it is useful to give more detailed explanations of why safety rules need to be applied, as children can better apply guidelines they understand. For example, children at a local primary school were told that they must not pick younger children up in the playground. Children of 7 and 8 were able to understand that a 4- or 5-year-old could be badly hurt if accidentally dropped by an older child. Children can also understand better why they need to wear safety belts in cars, helmets for bike riding and roller-blading and why road safety is so important. Children of this age may benefit not only from often-repeated verbal guidelines from adults, but also from topics or games which highlight particular safety issues. Praising children for remembering and applying safety rules will reinforce the child's careful behaviour.

Children of this age may need opportunities to demonstrate careful behaviour such as crossing the road without hand-holding, and later on, crossing the road alone. Adults need to give children opportunities to rely on their own judgement while maintaining an appropriate level of supervision. This can be difficult to judge at times as children vary greatly in their behaviour. It is important to remember that any child can forget or ignore safety issues if they are excited or ill or in a bad mood, so supervision should continue at all times.

Discussions about 'stranger danger' should continue and children should be helped to develop strategies for dealing with potential situations. For example, one small group of children were discussing what they would do if they became parted from their parents in a large indoor shopping centre. One child suggested that they ask a shopper for help, but another then posed the question 'What if they were a bad person and went off with you?' Eventually, the children agreed that the safe strategy would be to go in a shop and ask the person behind the counter for help, going right round the back of the counter to ensure they got the right person!

Helping children to increase their independence can be a difficult task at times and it can be tempting to avoid allowing children to try out new tasks because of safety concerns. Young children are at risk of accidents in the home particularly when they suddenly move to a new phase of development which carers are unprepared for. Children of 4 onwards are more vulnerable on the road as they practise physical skills such as running, jumping and bike riding (Thomas 1993). However, children need to learn safe behaviour gradually and to develop judgement about how they apply safety rules, in order to gain confidence and skills in dealing with the wider world.

109

Exercise 6

Taking into account the ages of the children you care for at work or on placement, write down the most significant factors in their stage of growth and development that affect their safety at this point in time. This could be learning to walk, putting objects in the mouth, using materials, outside play, learning to ride bikes, road safety, or trying out new activities such as using cutting tools, swimming and cooking. Make a note of how potential hazards are handled currently with the children in your work or placement setting. Are there any other ways of supporting the children to learn about safety issues? Could safety issues be handled differently to maximize the children's opportunity to learn and increase their levels of independence? Show your notes to a colleague or supervisor and ask for comments.

Accidents and Emergencies

Most accidents are preventable with careful planning and consideration of safety issues in the setting. However, accidents can happen at any time through unforeseen circumstances or events. The way in which you respond to an accident or emergency can make a significant difference to the outcome for the child. The most helpful responses are usually based on prior planning and preparation. The following guidelines cover some of the factors to consider:

- Ensure that children's records are accurate and up to date and that all relevant adults know of any specific risks to a child.
- Train in first aid or ensure that trained first aiders are available.
- Keep a fully equipped first aid box in an accessible location, and take a first aid kit in any vehicle used for transporting children.
- Know how to give medicine to a child where this has been agreed, e.g. inhalers.

- Keep emergency contact numbers at hand.
- Contact medical or emergency services if the child has a serious accident, has swallowed any potentially toxic substance, has breathing problems, is unresponsive, glazed, clammy or blue in the lips and nails or is bleeding heavily.
- Inform carers as soon as possible if there is serious cause for concern.
- Give clear accurate information when calling emergency services.
- Remain calm and reassure an ill or injured child.
- Trust your judgement and seek help or advice if you have concerns about a child's condition.
- Keep records of any accidents, however minor, in an accident book and make sure parents are informed.

To comply with expected standards there must be trained first aiders in every setting. You may want to consider seeking support to attend a reputable course or update your existing first aid skills through an approved refresher course. Your local Early Years Development and Childcare Partnership (EYDCP) should have details of appropriate courses and there may well be funding for this training. All early years workers should know what to do in a health emergency or when there is an accident.

Single carers should give particular attention to this aspect of safety as they may be the only adult around in a crisis. Childminders should plan what emergency action they could take if a child was injured or had a health emergency when in their care. It is a requirement of registration that all childminders have a first aid certificate at the time of registration or within six months of registration. Courses must be approved by OFSTED and the local authority. Information about courses can be found through the National Childminding Association (NCMA) (www.ncma.org.uk) or your local EYDCP.

Illness and Infection

Children are prone to a wide range of infections and illnesses, some of which are easily spread to other children in the same care situation. Colds and stomach upsets can pass rapidly around a group of children, if precautions are not taken to limit the spread of infection. The most important factor in reducing the spread of infection is to encourage parents to keep sick children at home. This is not as straightforward as it seems. A child may be only mildly unwell when she arrives in the setting, but she may become more ill later on in the day. A child with a cold may not feel particularly unwell, but still spread his virus to a range of other children and adults. Parents should be given clear guidelines about when it is inappropriate to bring a child to the setting and any concerns should be discussed with parents as soon as possible. We cannot prevent some bacterial and viral infections being passed on, but there are ways of limiting this:

- Ensure that hands are washed after children have used the toilet and before eating or touching food.
- Keep equipment and toys clean.
- Ensure the environment is clean and well-ventilated.
- Encourage children to use tissues for runny noses and sneezes and to cover their mouths when coughing.
- Be careful to follow hygiene rules when handling dirty nappies or wiping bottoms.
- Ensure that food and drinks are kept refrigerated and that food spills are cleaned up immediately.
- Clean and cover cuts and grazes.
- Seek medical advice and contact parents if a child becomes very ill while in your care.

Meningitis

Perhaps the most important illness to be aware of is meningitis, because it can develop so rapidly. Symptoms vary and can be different in young children and babies. In general, if the child has a bad headache, neck pain, a rash that does not disappear when pressed (use a glass), vomiting and an aversion to light, then you should contact the medical services immediately. Babies may be grumpy or hard to settle, while young children may be irritable. Medical centres and doctors' surgeries have leaflets that give clear advice about meningitis, which are useful to keep on hand for reference. As with all concerns about a child's health, seek medical advice if you are in any doubt and contact the parents.

Think *A Chance to Think*

Perhaps the most important method of ensuring that you respond well to any accident, emergency or health crisis involving the child or children in your care is forward planning. Knowledge of first aid and the symptoms of different childhood illnesses can be invaluable in reducing the impact of a crisis in the care of a child. All settings should have emergency procedures, which should be known to and followed by all practitioners in the setting. All accidents, emergencies or other safety issues should be recorded promptly, the appropriate person should be contacted (e.g. manager, supervisor, coordinator) and parents should be informed as soon as possible.

1 Check the emergency procedures or guidelines relevant to your setting, including who should be informed of any problem.
2 Check any requirements or guidelines on record-keeping in respect of accidents, emergencies or illness in your setting.
3 Draw an action plan of the areas you feel you need to know more about in terms of first aid, symptoms of illness or emergency procedures. Discuss this plan with a colleague or supervisor.

112
____

Abuse of Children

Early Years Practitioners and Child Abuse

Every early years worker has a responsibility to contribute to keeping children safe from abuse and neglect. For the majority of early years workers, this aspect of caring for children is both distressing and anxiety provoking. However, without the support of adults around them, children may continue to suffer abuse or neglect over a long period of time. Every year about 80 children die at the hands of their parents or carers and many more suffer physical injury and emotional damage, which in some cases can last for their lifetime. No one wants to believe that the children in their care are being abused, but a willingness to accept that abuse does take place, and that parents from all walks of life and economic backgrounds can be abusive, is the first step in protecting children. Recent tragic child deaths such as those of Victoria Climbie and Lauren Wright have highlighted the failure of individual practitioners to recognize the indicators of abuse and the poor levels of communication between agencies involved in providing services to children in terms of child protection issues. Failure of accountability and lack of information-sharing also contribute to these tragedies.

Child abuse is often categorized into physical, emotional, sexual abuse and neglect. However, many children are abused across these categories. For example, physically abused children are often neglected and sexually abused children often suffer mainly from the emotional damage inflicted on them by their abuser. The categories are useful for analysing abuse, but are hard to define due to the complex nature of child abuse and the unclear distinctions between abuse and non-abuse in some parental behaviour. For example, smacking is still considered an acceptable form of punishment of children in British society. But when does smacking become beating? How hard does a parent have to hit a child before this action is deemed abusive? Similarly, it can be hard to establish that emotional abuse and neglect have taken place in some cases, as the indicators often appear over long periods of time and the causes of these may be unclear.

All early years workers have a responsibility to be aware of the Area Child Protection Procedures, which outline the duties of everyone involved with children in a particular geographical area in cases of suspected abuse. Copies of these procedures should be available in nurseries, schools and other group settings and copies are also available in the local library. All early years settings and schools should also have their own child protection procedures, which outline the responsibilities of early years practitioners in the child protection process. Schools may also have copies of LEA procedures. It is important to ensure that all practitioners are familiar with the procedures and access relevant training where possible. All settings should have an individual who is responsible for child protection issues and who is trained in this area. Schools are required to have a child protection liaison teacher (a designated teacher) who acts as a coordinator and source of advice and support when suspected abuse arises.

For the majority of early years workers the main duty is to ensure that any concerns or suspicions about possible child abuse are passed on promptly to the appropriate person. In an institutional setting, this will be a supervisor or manager. Childminders should report concerns to their support workers. Any early years worker can pass concerns direct to the local authority social services department, but it is usual to follow agreed procedures within the workplace first. Students should discuss any concerns with their workplace supervisor or college tutor (in strictest confidence).

There are many reasons not to report abuse, including fear of being wrong and causing problems for parents, that the child may be removed into care or that there will be reprisals from the parents. Media reports during the 1980s and 1990s sometimes gave the impression that innocent parents are regularly separated from their children by over-zealous social workers. In fact, in most cases children are not removed from their families, and when they are, the majority go home within a short period of time. Support for families can be provided in many cases, to alleviate stress and reduce the risk of abuse continuing to take place. Non-reporting of abuse can result in a child continuing to suffer abuse for years, or in the worst cases being severely injured or killed.

Recognizing Child Abuse

One of the common concerns on child abuse courses is the fear of confusing the normal everyday bumps and bruises a child receives with the indicators of physical abuse. The simple answer to this concern is that you can probably not be entirely sure whether a child's injuries are accidental or not. However, your responsibilities do not include 'diagnosing' abuse. They do include reporting concerns about a child, often built up over a period of time through observation and listening which often include a whole range of physical and behavioural signs and symptoms which add up to a disturbing picture.

Sometimes children quite simply tell you that they are being abused and when this happens you need to listen and make a record of what the child said as soon as possible. It is important when a child makes a disclosure to ensure that you do not ask a lot of leading questions, such as, 'Did your dad hit you?' Instead, listen to the child carefully and offer reassurance and comfort. Never promise the child confidentiality, as you will have to share the child's conversation with colleagues and child protection social workers.

Indicators of possible abuse can often have other explanations, which would account for the injury or behaviour. It is your knowledge of the child that can help to unravel whether concerns are genuine or not, taking into account the child's circumstances and the explanations for the sign or symptom given by the child and/or parent. Possible indicators of abuse include:

- Bruises, cuts and other physical injuries on parts of the body where accidental injuries are unlikely to occur, for example soft tissues such as the thighs, buttocks or cheeks.
- Implausible or conflicting explanations for injuries from the parents and the child.
- Repeated injuries which seem unusual for the reasons given above.
- Changes in behaviour or persistently difficult behaviour including aggression, withdrawal, regression, distress, fear of adults or inability to engage in activities.
- Persistent sexualized behaviour that seems inappropriate for the child's age and understanding, such as sexual advances to adults or other children.
- Noticeable developmental delays for which there are no other explanations and which may include poor weight gain, lack of progress towards 'milestones', apathetic responses and 'failure to thrive'.
- Low self-esteem, lack of confidence and poor social skills.

Many behavioural indicators may have other explanations in terms of conflict or stress in a child's life, for example divorce or separation of parents, reconstituted families, birth of another child into the family or illness or death of a family member. Physical indicators may also have other explanations. It is important to use your judgement and knowledge of the child to determine whether you have grounds for concern and to talk over your observations with a colleague in strictest confidence. Asking yourself the following questions may help to clarify the issues:

- Have a colleague or I had concerns about this child or another child in the same family previously?
- Is there a known history of child abuse within this family?
- Does the explanation for the indicators make sense and do the explanations of the child and parents tally and remain consistent?

- Are there other stress factors in the family that I know of and could these explain the child's behaviour or condition?
- Has the child or any other child in the family said anything that has caused concerns?
- How do the child and parents respond to each other?

You also need to discuss your concerns with an appropriate person before taking any action. This could be the child protection liaison worker/teacher or your manager or supervisor. If you work alone, you may need to talk to someone in social services, making it clear that you are seeking advice, rather than making a referral at that point. If a referral should be made, the duty social worker will advise you of this.

Always try to make a note of any concerns you have and why you have them, at the earliest possible point. Remember that records should be accurate and should avoid judgements or speculation and include only facts. Concerns should be shared with parents wherever possible. Records should be kept confidentially.

Think — A Chance to Think

In any child abuse case there are a number of procedures which will be followed and it is important to be aware of these and ensure that you contribute to protecting the child within the bounds of your job role. However, it can seem sometimes that the child gets 'lost' in the procedures. One of your roles may be to provide continuity and support for the child during a stressful period, while suspected abuse is investigated and acted upon.

Exercise 8

1 Find out what the child protection procedures are in respect of your job role or work or placement setting. If you are not sure about any aspect of the procedures ask a colleague or supervisor.
2 Write down how you can offer support to a child and the family during a child protection enquiry and the problems you may encounter in this role. Compare your answers to the sample answers in the Appendix.

Reporting Abuse

If you have reached the conclusion, possibly after discussion with a colleague, that you have a sufficient level of concern about a child to take action, then it is important that you follow any workplace procedures in reporting your concerns. Schools and some nurseries will have a child protection liaison teacher through whom all reports of suspected abuse should be channelled. Some private nurseries may have agreements with the local social services department about how suspected abuse is reported. Pre-schools and out-of-school settings may all have agreed procedures about what to do if abuse is suspected. Check the procedures in your workplace and ensure that you work within them. Reports should be clear, including the child's personal details, information about who cares for the child, any information you have about siblings and any special factors such as disabilities or English as a second language. Causes for concern should be recorded factually, without opinion or attempts to apportion blame. Whatever the procedures you follow, the report will go to a child protection social worker, who will investigate the concerns. In general, the setting is expected to make parents aware that a referral is being made unless contacting the parents may put the child at greater risk.

What Happens Next?

The investigation will establish if there are reasons to be concerned about the child and will include interviews with the family, the child according to her age and any other professional involved with the child. A child protection case conference will be called if cause for concern is established. This is a meeting of all professionals involved with the child, which normally involves parents. The child's circumstances will be discussed and recommendations made to protect the child if necessary. These will be written into a child protection plan, which may involve a range of workers supporting and monitoring the child's progress. You may be asked to attend the case conference, in which case you will need to have kept an accurate set of records containing any relevant information about the child. If your level of involvement has reached this stage, you may need to seek personal support from colleagues or supervisors, as child protection processes can be distressing and stressful for those involved. Strictest confidentiality must be maintained.

It is possible that the child protection case conference will recommend care proceedings under the Children Act 1989 or that the child is removed from home before the case conference on an emergency protection order, if the child is considered to be in immediate danger of harm.

You may be involved in supporting the child and family as part of the child protection plan, either through monitoring the child's condition and behaviour or offering direct support to the children and family. If this is the case you need to be careful to keep accurate records and to report any concerns to the key worker, who is usually the social worker.

The Practitioner's Role in Developing Safety

Children need to feel (as well as be) both psychologically and physically safe within the setting. Children who are bullied; harassed because of other's perceptions of their difference; discriminated against because of colour, culture, language or religion; called names or excluded from play and friendships may not feel either physically or psychologically safe within the early years setting. Developing a safe environment for all children depends largely on the attitudes, behaviour and approaches of the practitioners within that setting.

There are a number of approaches that can support the development of a safe environment for all children. They include:

- Developing respectful and supportive relationships between staff.
- Good teamwork, communication and coordination between staff.
- Good communication and supportive relationships with parents.
- Positive and constructive approaches to behaviour management.
- Firm, fair handling of any behavioural problems, bullying or discrimination.
- Warm and respectful relationships with children.
- Strong positive representations of all ethnic groups within the setting.
- Conversation about the importance of sharing, support, anti-discriminatory behaviour and respect for all.
- Activities that promote learning and development for all.
- Support for children who need help accessing play, friendships or structured activities.

The ethos of the setting should be clear to all parents, children and visitors through written policies, conversation, and the attitudes, behaviour and demeanour of staff and children (see also 'Creating a Safe and Supportive Environment for All Children' in Chapter 4).

Records

Children's individual records should be accurate and up-to-date, ensuring that any important information about the child's health or well-being is included. This information should be made available to staff on a need-to-know basis and otherwise kept confidential (see Chapter 8). Any concerns about the child should be recorded in consultation with any other relevant staff, and these concerns should generally be shared with parents. Parents should always be informed of any event which may affect the child's health or well-being, even very minor accidents. This can be done orally, but is usually done by giving the parent a note or sending a note with the child. The value of written communications is that they ensure that parents have received the information and that they are aware of any potential problem for the child. For example, a child who has bumped his head could develop the symptoms of mild concussion later on at home. Written communications also help to protect the early years worker against any allegations by the parents. For example, if the child has a series of injuries which are not explained to the parents, they may become concerned about the standard of care in the setting.

Records should also be kept of any agreements with the parents about administering medicines to children such as asthma inhalers or antibiotics. Notes should be kept of the time any medicine is administered and any problem that may have arisen with giving the medicine.

It is particularly important to keep records of any concerns you may have about the child's condition which may relate to suspected abuse. Data protection law requires that all records should be accurate: therefore, any recording of concerns about suspected abuse needs to be factual and objective, rather than emotional or accusatory. Ideally, the contents of such records should be shared with parents, although this should be discussed with the appropriate person first and it should be considered whether discussion with parents may put the child more at risk. Any decision to record concerns about suspected abuse should be done in conjunction with a supervisor, colleague or other appropriate person. All such records should be kept highly confidential and not discussed with any other person, except on a need-to-know basis.

Records should be kept in a safe place, which is inaccessible to others and should be shared only on a need-to-know basis. Childminders need to give particular consideration to storing records safely and maintaining confidentiality.

Conclusions

Physical safety is important to children, but children need to feel emotionally safe as well. We have already discussed the way in which children need to develop towards independence by taking some limited risks and learning to think for themselves. It is always important to balance safety issues with the child's need to grow and learn by exploring new environments.

Early years practitioners have a significant role in developing safe environments that support all children's physical and psychological safety. Your attitude and behaviour are vitally important in creating a safe ethos and role modelling acceptable behaviour to the children.

REFERENCES AND FURTHER READING

Equal Opportunities Commission www.eoc.org.uk.

Health and Safety Executive www.hse.gov.uk.

Kay, J. (2003) *Protecting Children: A Practical Guide* (2nd edn). London: Continuum.

Lindon, J. and Lindon, L. (1993) *Caring for the Under-8s: Working to Achieve Good Practice*. London: Macmillan.

O'Hagan, M. (1997) *Geraghty's Caring for Children* (3rd edn). London: Ballière Tindall.

Tassoni, P. (1998) *Child Care and Education*. Oxford: Heinemann.

Tassoni, P. and Beith, K. (1999) *Nursery Nursing: A Guide to Work in Early Years*. Oxford: Heinemann.

Taylor, J. and Woods, M. (eds) (1998) *Early Childhood Studies: An Holistic Introduction*. London: Arnold.

Thomas, E. (1993) 'Accidents in childhood', in E. A. Glosper and A. Tucker (eds) *Advances in Child Health Nursing*. London: Scutori.

7 Working With Parents and Other Professionals

INTRODUCTION

No one in early years education and care works alone. Children are not cared for in isolation from their families or the local community. Whether you are a child's most significant carer or you are part of a team with a group of children, you will always be working in partnership with other adults who have a place in the child's life. In most cases the most important people you will work with are parents or carers. However, you may at times find yourself working as part of a multidisciplinary team involving health visitors, social workers, teachers and other school staff and possibly other relatives and friends of the child and the family. The quality of the relationship between the child's different carers and interested adults is a crucial determinant of the quality of the care and education received by the child. A good working relationship with parents means that you will communicate about the child's needs and any concerns about the child. If there are problems, they are more likely to be resolved quickly and effectively. The child will be cared for and educated in complementary ways at home and in the setting.

Working together is a major theme in the early years, reflecting concerns about the poor standards and waste of resources which can result from fragmented, uncoordinated arrangements. The conflicts that can occasionally arise between different individuals involved with a child can be very damaging to the child and the quality of his care and education. Working together can sometimes be more difficult than it seems. The concept of partnership depends on some level of agreement about work practices and the best interests of the child. In order to achieve this agreement, there often has to be some level of compromise and striving to reach common ground. As one of the professionals involved with the child, the early years worker has a responsibility to work towards achieving good relationships with parents and other professionals and establishing effective communication.

Essentially, working together is about putting the child's welfare first – above professional and personal differences and other considerations. The child's needs should always be considered as the most important factor when developing working partnerships with parents and other professionals.

Working with Parents

Working with parents is a key area of good practice for early years workers. Often this good practice is expressed through informal or casual every day contact with the parents of the children you work with. There may also be more formal contact if there is a problem or concern, or some difficulty which needs resolving.

The next few sections look at parents and the parenting role, how parents might try to meet their children's needs, and the problems and anxieties that many parents experience trying to achieve good standards of care and education for their children.

What is a Parent?

Working with parents is one of the skills that early years workers need to develop in order to ensure that their practice meets the standards required in early years settings today and in the future. But who are 'the parents'? As already mentioned in the Preface, the term 'parent' is used to describe the main carer or carers of the child. This could be birth parents, adoptive parents, grandparents or other relatives, single parents, step-parents or guardians. Basically, the term 'parents' describes the adults with whom the child lives and/or those who have parental responsibility for the child. In some cases, this may be more than one person or set of people living in more than one household. In other cases there may be shared parental responsibility between parents and the local authority, as when the child is subject to a care order within the Children Act 1989.

Why Do We Need to Work with Parents?

You may be asking why working with parents is a good practice issue – what are the benefits of working together? Parents are the most significant adults in children's lives. They have intimate knowledge and understanding of the child and are the most influential factor in the child's early development. Children learn a wide range of different knowledge and behaviour from parents, including how to be part of a family. Early years workers need to develop good relationships and effective partnerships with parents in order to ensure that children receive care and education that is coordinated between different settings and adults.

Whatever your early years setting or existing level of involvement with parents, it is important to examine the quality of the relationship you have with them, as part of your continuing process of developing good practice.

Working together is a duty of early years workers under legislation relating to child protection, education and children with special needs. For example, area child protection procedures and the Department of Health guidelines 'Working Together to Safeguard Children' (1999) emphasize the importance of multidisciplinary cooperation and coordination to protect children from abuse successfully.

It may be easy to assume sometimes that parents are uncaring or indifferent to their child's needs and to respond to them in ways that convey this. Or you may feel that some parents challenge your practice and 'interfere' with the service you offer. Dealing with these feelings and developing a more positive approach to parental involvement may be hard work, but can have benefits for the child, the parent and the practitioner.

The value of developing effective partnerships with parents is now widely recognized as a significant factor in the welfare of the child, and research findings support this view. The 'Curriculum Guidance for the Foundation Stage' (QCA, 2000), 'Birth to Three Matters' (Sure Start, 2003), the Children Act 1989 and the Special Educational Needs Code of Practice (DfES, 2001) all emphasize the value of working with parents to support children's care and education and promote their learning and development.

The basic premise of working together is that children will benefit from a co-ordinated approach to their care that is free of conflict and in which the various carers support each other to care to a high standard, and where all involved are working toward common goals based on the child's best interests. In other words: 'Parents and professionals can help children separately or they can work together to the greater benefit of the children' (Athey 1990, quoted in Whalley 1997, p. 1). Research in schools shows that children do benefit from such collaboration. Bastiani (1995) states that 'there is a clear argument, supported by extensive and convincing evidence, that the most effective education occurs when families and schools work together, as part of a shared enterprise' (quoted in Taylor and Woods, 1998, p. 219).

Working together with parents can help you to understand individual children better by finding out more information about their lives outside the early years context. Knowing more of the concerns and problems the children might have and the things that are important to them can help to ensure you are more sensitive and responsive to their needs. In cases where the child is from a different culture or background from yours or the child has physical or learning disabilities, there may be even more reason to value opportunities to discover more of the child's history and circumstances and to share thoughts and ideas with parents on how best to meet the child's needs.

Parents can benefit from collaboration with early years workers in a variety of ways. They may get important insights into their child's ability and behaviour outside the home. They may get positive feedback from the early years worker about the quality of their parenting and support for any difficulties they may be concerned about. They may also develop ideas and strategies for promoting and supporting their child's play and learning and for dealing with difficult behaviour. The skilled early years worker can act as a role model for parents who need support to develop their parenting skills.

As an early years worker, you may now be asking 'How do we benefit from working with parents?' It may seem from your point of view that although collaboration with parents is a positive step to take, for the worker it involves a lot of extra time and effort. But working with parents can both enhance your working life and improve the quality of service you offer to the children. Taking time to communicate with parents can give you a better understanding of the child. You may learn from the parent's skills and knowledge in childcare and education and share strategies for dealing with problems or difficult behaviour. You may find that parents have a great deal of practical help to offer, and last but not least, you may get some of that rare but precious positive feedback that we all need at times.

A Chance to Think

Concentrating on the benefits of working together can help to improve your approach to parents. By appreciating the advantages of cooperation, parents can be valued more and early years workers can make a genuine commitment to equality in partnership with them.

Exercise 1

IAN

Ian is 2. He has just started at your nursery for two days a week to fit in with his parents' working hours. Ian is the first child with Down's syndrome you have had at the nursery. When his parents first approached the nursery, you spent quite a lot of time talking to them about Ian's special needs, as well as his more general likes and dislikes, habits and abilities. These discussions helped you a lot to understand more about Ian and how to best care for him and support his learning. The parents seemed very reassured about your plans for Ian and were helpful in settling him into nursery and communicating any problems he was having to you.

One of the staff at the nursery has obtained a place on a course about learning to care for children with disabilities, and she is sharing the ideas and information she has acquired with the rest of the team. This is helping you to understand the impact of Down's syndrome on the child in the family and the wider context. Ian has settled into nursery and is responding well to both staff and the other children. His parents continue to share information with you about Ian and you report back on his progress and the development of new skills. Recently, Ian has added an extra day to his time at nursery and this transition went very smoothly.

1 Write down how you think Ian, his parents and the nursery staff may be benefiting from the positive relationship between nursery staff and the parents.
2 How might the relationship be useful if difficulties arose, for example, if Ian was subject to name-calling by other children?

Compare your answers with the sample answers in the Appendix.

The Role of Parents

In order to understand and value the role of the parent in an equal partnership, it is important to give some thought to the parenting role and what it entails. Parents take on a task that not only is overwhelming in range and scope, but also lasts forever and comes with huge emotional, physical and financial demands attached to it. It is a role that is frequently discussed, often criticized and rarely valued. The parental role is not a highly valued or rewarded one in society as a whole, but despite this, parents are urged to find more time for their children, to supervise them better, to help more with their education and to ensure they grow up as well-rounded responsible citizens.

Parents are subject to a barrage of conflicting advice about what to feed their children, how to discipline them, how to help them learn and how to detect and avoid the myriad of pitfalls open to young children. Very rarely do parents get praise for the tasks they perform or acknowledgement that they are doing a good job in difficult circumstances. As a result, lack of confidence is often a problem, particularly for new parents and parents who are isolated from support. Many feel uncertain about whether the parenting skills they have are adequate or whether their child-rearing practices are in the best interests of the child.

Think *A Chance to Think*

Exploring the role of the parent in more detail can be very helpful in reaching a better understanding of the parents and children you work with. Parenting is not a single task, but a series of complex linked activities that involve a high level of emotional commitment, physical energy, organization and stamina. Parents often go unrewarded for long periods of time and may have little time for themselves, partners or friends. Many parents will tell of times in their children's early years where they have felt desperate for a break or extra support just to carry on coping. Child-rearing is often only one of the roles parents have to fulfil. As increasing numbers of women take up employment, many families have to manage an exhausting schedule of work and childcare responsibilities.

Exercise 2

1 Write a list of all the tasks and roles a parent may have to perform in an average week.
2 List all the different aspects of the child's life that a parent will have to be aware of and respond to.
3 Think about the work in the home that having children creates, and the work outside the home that the majority of parents do.
4 Think about the financial demands on families with young children and the stresses these could place on families on low incomes.
5 Think about the emotional demands of parenting and how relentless these can be at times.
6 Use your own experience if you are a parent and discuss your list with other parents, including some parents of children you work with, if possible. Bear in mind the additional difficulties that may be faced by parents of children with physical or learning disabilities or parents living within a different culture to their own.

The Needs of Children

In order to explore the task of parenting it may be helpful to look at the needs children have that parents try to meet.

• **Basic physical care** such as food, drink, warmth, hygiene, shelter and protection.
• **Warmth and affection** including cuddles and kisses, appreciation, time and effort, patience and tolerance, praise and admiration, a sense of belonging.
• **Emotional security** including harmony, stability and continuity of care, routines and predictability in daily care, consistency in style and approach of care, lack of anxiety.
• **Support and stimulation to achieve potential** such as play, social opportunities, educational opportunities, praise for achievements, encouragement to develop skills
• **Guidance and control** to help the child learn acceptable behaviour, to develop moral sense and a regard for others and which offers the child a good model of behaviour.
• **Methods of discipline** which are suitable to the child's age and understanding, which help the child understand how to behave differently and which are not cruel or humiliating.
• **Responsibility** within the boundaries of age and ability to build confidence and a sense of independence, to help the child learn to make decisions and develop good judgement which is encouraged and consolidated with praise.

- **Protection** from physical harm or danger, providing good supervision and increasing independence within the limits of the child's age and ability.

(with thanks to Cooper 1985, quoted in Pugh et al. 1994, p. 50)

Clearly these are ideals and not all parents (or early years workers) can meet all of these needs all of the time. However, the list gives us an idea of the range of areas that parents focus on during their day-to-day activities and routines with children. It gives an idea of the parameters of the parenting task.

How Parents Meet their Children's Needs

How parents set about meeting the needs of their children will vary a great deal and may depend on a number of different social, cultural and economic factors. Parenting is not a skill we are born with, although we are predisposed to care for our children and develop a loving relationship with them through the process of bonding and attachment. Parenting skills are learned from a range of sources, including our own experiences of being parented and the cultural norms of parenting that we absorb through our own process of socialization. This is not necessarily a conscious process. For example, it is a basic rule of safety in one family that children should never run with lollipops in their mouths. This rule has been passed down to the next generation of children without any consideration of whether it is a valid concern or major safety issue, simply because it was absorbed as part of the mother's mental picture of good parenting practices. Factors that affect how and to what extent parents can meet the needs of their children might include:

- **Cultural and social norms of child rearing** – the types of childcare practices which are normal within a particular culture or class, such as style of dress, hygiene practices, food and eating habits.
- **Parents' own experience of being parented** – the ideas and convictions that parents have about parenting which they have learned from their own experience as children, for example methods of discipline, levels of physical contact, expectations of the child, safety issues.
- **Current wisdom** – the ideas and beliefs about parenting that parents have learned from professional advice, books, magazines and television, such as what constitutes a good diet, the possible side-effects of immunization.
- **Parents' economic situation** – the extent to which financial limitations affect the ways in which parents can meet the child's material needs and the impact of financial worries on the parents' stress levels, health and well-being.
- **Environment and living conditions** – the housing and facilities available to the family, for example the amount of indoor space, whether there is a garden, easy access to parks and other leisure facilities, access to schools, nursery,

playgroup, after-school care and medical services, levels of security within the neighbourhood.

- **Levels of support** – the extent to which parents can access formal and informal support systems in their local community, such as childcare facilities, contact groups for parents, family and friends, specialist support for health or other problems.
- **Parents' social situation** – the extent to which different types of parents are accepted and supported within their own communities, for example the impact of racism and/or cultural isolation, the extent of support for female and male single parents, gay and lesbian parents and parents with mental health problems.
- **Family relationships** – the quality of relationships within the family and whether these are subject to stress, such as family conflict, abuse and domestic violence, poor communications between parents.
- **Disability or illness** – the extent to which the disability or health problems of any family member can limit the family's ability to cope, for example the chronic ill-health of a parent, mental health problems of a parent, disability or learning difficulties of a child in the family.

A Chance to Think

Parents' circumstances may have a profound impact on their ability to meet their children's needs on a consistent basis. Many parents struggle to cope with a range of problems and difficulties as well as providing good quality care to their children. For some parents the struggle to cope can be overwhelming and the care of their children suffers because of this. Loving and caring parents can sometimes fail to provide an acceptable standard of care for their children.

Exercise 3

Read the short case studies below and for each one describe how the parent's circumstances may affect their ability to meet their children's needs. You may want to refer back to the list of children's needs above. Compare your answers with the sample answers in the Appendix.

HOWARD

Howard is 2 years old. He lives with his mother, who has been diagnosed as having clinical depression. Howard's mother separated from his father before Howard was born and there is no contact. Howard's mother has no friends or family in the area they live in and they do not go to the local playgroup or use the local park. In fact, most days they stay in and some days Howard's mother does not have the energy to get them dressed or cook food or play with Howard. Sometimes she just lies on the settee and does not speak.

SARA

Sara's parents have worked hard to try to provide Sara (aged 6) and her brother and sister with a good standard of living. Sara's father works long hours in the day and comes home exhausted. Sara's mother works evening and afternoon shifts in a supermarket. They are trying to pay off debts and keep payments up on a big mortgage. They do not have much time together or to do things with the children. Both are worried about money and this leads to a lot of rows and occasional screaming matches.

DONOVAN

Donovan's mother died when he was 6 months old, and his father is raising him and his older sister alone. His father has had to give up his job to do this and they live on benefits on a pre-war council estate. Donovan's father was a physically and emotionally abused child. He was brought up in the care system and he has no contact with his extended family because of this. He very much wants to parent his children in a different way from his own upbringing, but he does not seek support or advice because he thinks that social services will get involved and he will lose the children.

CARL

Carl was born with cerebral palsy. He is now 2 years old. His parents have just had another baby, who does not sleep well and who is very colicky at times. Carl's father works shifts and his mother is at home with the children most of the time. Carl's father has started to spend more time outside the home on top of his work hours. He has never talked to anyone about his feelings about Carl and he seems to be avoiding contact with the new baby. Carl's mother thinks he might be having a relationship with another woman.

JASMINE

Jasmine is 3. She attends the nursery attached to the local school. She is one of a very few African Caribbean children in the school and community. Jasmine has been called names at school and this has upset her. When her mother complained, she did not feel that the school took the problem seriously. Some of her neighbours are very unfriendly to her and others ignore the family. Jasmine's mother and father do not have local friends and are not part of the community activities that go on in the neighbourhood.

Parenting Skills and Dispositions

It is important to remember that the majority of parents are trying to do the difficult task of parenting as well as they can, sometimes in far from ideal circumstances. Parenting is not only about a range of tasks and abilities, but also about the intimate knowledge and understanding of the child that only a parent has. It is about shared history, shared pleasures and a mutual sense of belonging. For many parents, the role of parenting brings enormous satisfaction and great joy at times. Before we go on to explore how early years workers can establish genuine and supportive partnerships with parents, it may be helpful to consider the skills required by parents (and early years workers too) and how these contribute to good standards of childcare and education.

The range and type of parenting skills required during childhood are infinite, as any parent knows. They change according to the age and ability of the child and family circumstances. Part of being a parent is the touching trust that children place in you to be able to change a bike tyre, bake a cake, mend toys, produce meals for your child and four friends in under ten minutes, know why the wind blows, how far the moon is away and why their best friend has fallen out with them. More general skills for parenting include the ability to:

- feel and show love and affection
- set limits and apply firm, consistent boundaries
- know or find out the stages a child goes through and be sensitive to changing needs
- show respect and regard for the child
- develop self-awareness and self-confidence
- be empathetic and see the world as the child might
- be patient, tolerant and kind
- give time, energy and commitment
- support the child in her chosen activities, share successes and problems
- sometimes be imaginative or funny or silly.

Parents may need help to develop some of these skills and apply them within their own families. Much of parenting is an automatic process, so recognizing the need to develop new skills for parenting may not be easy at times. Early years workers who take time to develop relationships with parents can support this process by acknowledging problems and acting as a role-model of good practice and a source of advice and support. It is also important that parents enjoy their children and have fun with them and avoid becoming over-anxious about whether they are doing a good job or not.

Partnership with Parents

The concept of working together with parents is based on a number of underlying principles – beliefs about the child and the parents and the role of the childcare worker in relation to these.

- Parents are the most important people in a child's life.

- Parents are experts on their own children.
- Parents are sometimes under a great deal of pressure from a range of sources.
- Some parents have few supports and struggle to cope.
- Parenting is a complex and demanding role requiring a wide range of skills.
- Parenting skills are not always easy to develop.
- External factors, such as a poor environment or poverty, can distract parents from the parenting role.
- The child's best interests will be better met if parents and childcare workers work together.
- There are many different ways of parenting, some more successful than others.
- Cultural differences in parenting are an important part of celebrating and maintaining cultural identity.

131

Think *A Chance to Think*

Working with parents is not always easy. In order to be successful in establishing and maintaining partnerships with parents which really work to improve services to children, you need to have considered some of the principles underlying the need to work together. Parents have not always been considered partners with early years services and this has sometimes resulted in negative outcomes for the child.

Exercise 4

Read the case study and answer the questions below. Ask your colleagues if they share your views. Compare your answers with the sample answers in the Appendix.

DREW

Drew attended a social services-sponsored day nursery place from the age of 12 months because of family problems that had badly affected his parents' relationship. Drew was 18 months old when his father received a caution for bruising him on the face. The father left the family home as part of the child protection plan for Drew. Drew's mother had two other children, including a 2-month-old baby. When she took Drew to nursery the day after the child protection case conference, staff found it difficult to know how to approach her. The next day Drew did not attend nursery. Eventually the social worker told staff that Drew's mother did not want to bring him to nursery because she thought the staff were looking down on her and thinking she was a bad parent.

1 What might be the impact on Drew and his family if he does not return to his nursery place?

2 Imagine you are Drew's mother. What practical problems might you be experiencing now? What feelings might you have about the situation you are in?

3 What sort of support could the nursery staff offer Drew and his family?

4 How could Drew's mother be encouraged to bring him to nursery again?

Woods (1998) summarizes the factors that need to be present in order to have effective home–school links. Adapted to take into account other forms of early years care and education settings, the list of factors leading to positive partnerships with parents might read like this:

- planned and integrated approach to establishing and maintaining partnerships with parents
- involving parents in decision-making
- acknowledging parents' skills and abilities and inviting them to share these
- welcoming parents and helping them feel at ease in the setting
- good communication and information sharing
- sharing responsibility and accountability.

In addition, it is important to try and see events and actions from the parents' point of view and to recognize how daunting the childcare setting, and the professionals within it, can be to many parents.

Not all parents will want to get involved. For some, early years settings are places where the child goes to be cared while the parent is elsewhere. For others, getting involved requires levels of energy and confidence that they do not possess at that point in time. However, many parents might like to have more knowledge and understanding of their child's experiences while in your care.

Achieving partnership with parents involves some genuine readjustments in order to accommodate their views, opinions and involvement. It is not too difficult to play lip-service to partnership without giving up any of the control in your setting. However, this could be frustrating for all those involved. Looking at the points on the list above can help to start to identify areas for change or development in order to work towards effectively involving parents.

Planned and Integrated Approach to Establishing and Maintaining Partnerships with Parents

Obviously the range of areas in which you can plan parental involvement depends on your work setting and the expectations of that setting. However, it is important to think through all aspects of potential parental involvement in order to ensure that all possible areas have been considered. Major areas of involvement, which should be considered in all settings, are settling children in and moving them on. For example, it is important to plan your first meeting with parents. Think about the sorts of concerns that parents might have about leaving their child, especially if it is for the first time. Think about how these concerns might make them feel and what sort of anxieties they might have. Try to write down a list of feelings and concerns the parents might have. Then write down the concerns you might have yourself. These might include normal anxieties about whether you will like the child and the parents, or worries about whether you will be able to meet the specific needs of a particular child.

By acknowledging that you and the parents come together for the first time with different sets of concerns, you may be able to think of strategies to put them at their ease and make sure the right sorts of information are exchanged. Parents need to feel welcomed by you from the start, whatever the setting. Careful planning of initial contact can establish the foundations of a good relationship. Planning how parental feedback can be obtained is also important. Will this be done formally or informally? What sort of time and space can you make to ensure parents have the opportunity to express any worries or concerns? Have you somewhere private and quiet to talk to parents? You also need to think about how you are going to give feedback to parents on their child's progress and share any of your concerns. Planning opportunities to confer with parents ensures that communication will actually take place.

Other areas to plan are how, and to what extent, parents can be involved in day-to-day activities and decision-making processes, and how you might utilize parents' skills and abilities.

Involving Parents in Decision-making

Parents can be involved at many levels of decision-making, including choosing activities for the children, planning the layout of the setting, choosing toys and materials, trips out and other resources. For example, at a primary school some of the parents attended a meeting to discuss new playground equipment for the nursery, for which money had been raised. The parents looked at catalogues and discussed with nursery staff and the headteacher the best way of spending the money to benefit the majority of children. Eventually, a general agreement about the type of equipment wanted was made and a small committee was chosen to work out the details. Parents were able to understand the different issues involved in funding school equipment and the pitfalls of buying resources that could be funded from other sources. The nursery bought equipment that was valued by parents and this strengthened the sense of positive partnership between parents and staff. It also fuelled enthusiasm for a further round of fundraising.

However, the main area of decision-making that parents are involved in is how their own child will be cared for and educated outside the home. Not all parents have a choice, but many will do a lot of thinking and research before deciding the best type of care and education for their child. It is important to acknowledge parents' requirements for their children and to try to meet them within the setting. These could be centred around food, sleep, learning activities, areas for development, hygiene practices and many other areas where cultural and individual differences in practices need to be considered sensitively and positively. If there are conflicts between the parent's requirements for the child and policy in your setting, these need to be discussed openly and honestly and the outcomes agreed. Read the following case study and think about how it was handled.

JENNY

Case Study

Jenny, who was 2 years old, attended a family centre as part of her placement agreement as a foster child. One of the concerns about Jenny was that she did not eat well and she was small and underweight. Staff at the centre had a remit to help Jenny to eat better by providing stimulating activities and feeding her lunch. Jenny arrived every morning clutching a half-eaten bag of crisps. In addition she had often had sweets on the way to the centre. Her foster family ate a lot of sweets and crisps and did not consider these to affect appetite, but Jenny never ate more than a few mouthfuls of lunch.

Jenny's key worker talked to the foster parent, praising her work with Jenny and the progress she had made. She encouraged her to stay at the centre with Jenny and join in activities. Eventually she suggested to the foster carer that Jenny had a small appetite and could not manage her dinners because she had snacked in the morning. She asked if they could try cutting out the snacks for a week to see what happened. In the context of her good relationship with staff at the centre and the support they provided, the foster carer was not offended by the suggestion and the experiment was successful.

Acknowledging Parents' Skills and Abilities and Inviting Them to Share These

Parents have myriad skills, including caring for and educating their children! Early years providers can benefit enormously from finding out about parental skills and tapping into these. Whether it is parents with practical skills which they are willing to share or parents who are happy to come and join in existing activities, this is a resource that is often under-utilized. Fears that parents might take over or become too involved can influence the extent to which early years workers encourage their involvement. However, the following list of examples shows some of the skills and talents that parents can bring to a setting:

- A parent who planned and carried out landscaping in a school garden.

- A parent who helped the nursery to build up a stock of suitable second language books.
- Parents who supported the after-school club's trips out to local 'park ranger' events.
- Parents who read with reception class children regularly for one or two hours per week.
- A parent who helped the nursery to set up a display of African Caribbean food and cooking utensils.
- A parent who discussed the needs of blind children, from his own child's experience, with the local childminding group.

In order to find out what parents have to offer, make opportunities to talk to them about the areas they are interested in and the skills they have. These can be formal or informal, but depend on genuine interest from the practitioners. Parents need to be invited to share skills, whether to help out generally or offer a particular skill or piece of knowledge. Clearly the extent to which parents can be actively involved will depend on the setting. Nurseries, schools, pre-schools and other group settings provide wider scope for involving parents, while other settings may be more limited. However, all parents can share their understanding of their own child's needs, or can be invited to discuss how to deal with particular behaviour or how to introduce different play activities. For example, sharing information with parents about different strategies for improving concentration skills in a child may result in improvements at home and in the setting.

Parents can be asked if they would like to

- help out generally in the setting
- talk to the children about a specific talent or interest
- join steering groups, governors or fundraising groups
- be involved in social events for parents.

In single carer settings these more formal levels of involvement clearly are not possible. However, it is important to find ways of making parents feel you are genuinely interested in what they have to offer.

Welcoming Parents and Helping Them Feel at Ease in the Setting

Pause for a moment and imagine you are a parent coming to visit the early years setting for the first time. The parent may encounter the following:

- professional, and often trained and qualified, early years workers with a wide range of experience

- an unfamiliar place in which their child is going to spend time without the parent
- an array of toys, activities and opportunities for experiences that the child may not get at home
- an unfamiliar set of routines which their child will learn and take part in
- images, language and other representations of a different culture from that of the parent and child.

It may feel very daunting to the most confident of parents to try to discuss how they feel about leaving their child in these circumstances. Parents may feel they have nothing to contribute or they may not think that their views and opinions have any value in the setting. In order to make parents feel welcome and comfortable some thought needs to go into both the physical environment and the way in which contact with parents is managed.

The setting needs to be accessible to parents both physically and psychologically. This means that parents should be able to come into the setting with smaller children and buggies. In institutional settings, signs should show new parents the way in, there should be a noticeboard with information and greetings on it and there should be displays of the children's work. In all settings parents should be greeted and made to feel welcome and time should be taken for a few words with them. Parents should not be made to feel as if they are being hustled back out of the door so you can get on with the business of the day.

For example, in one educare setting, the child attended daycare in the morning and nursery school in the afternoon. The daycare staff were not very welcoming and did not make much effort to talk to the parent in the mornings or greet him with a smile. The parent never really got beyond the door of the room. He was not invited to look at the activities prepared for the day or discuss his child's progress. When the parent collected his child from the nursery section, he was greeted warmly and shown the child's work or activities of the day. Staff were always willing to discuss the child's progress or any concerns the parent had. The staff praised the child in front of the parent, and talked about the strategies that they used to encourage the child's learning, particularly in his language development. They asked the parent's opinion and advice on this and other aspects of the child's development. As a result the parent did not feel confident in the daycare his child received and felt that it was of a lower standard than the nursery provision.

Other issues to consider are how parents will know 'who is who' in a setting with more than one worker (workers could wear name badges or there could be photos of staff on the wall) or how you address the parent (check whether it is first names or titles, whether the parent has a different name from the child and how to pronounce unfamiliar names).

Welcoming new parents can be particularly important in order to establish the basis for good rapport from the start.

Case Study

DAVEY

Jane and Philip wanted to find a nursery for their son Davey, who was rising 3. They felt that Davey needed some special care because of his slight hearing impairment and some general developmental delays. They had visited one or two nurseries (private and school) and talked to friends who used childminders about the benefits of this option. They then visited Minton Street Nursery. An appointment was made and the head of the nursery talked to the couple and Davey in her office. She discussed the nursery philosophy and routines, their approach to working with parents and children and the ways in which the child's progress was recorded and relayed to parents. Davey was encouraged to play with some toys in the office and the head took time to talk to him about what he was doing.

The head then showed Jane and Philip around the nursery. They saw a range of toys and equipment in use and a general sense of purposeful and enjoyable activity. The rooms were bright and welcoming, well laid out and with displays of the children's work in each. Staff were introduced and were warm and welcoming, keen to show Jane and Philip what they were doing with the children, and to answer any questions. The outside play area was attractive and well-equipped for a range of activities at different levels of ability. The foyer had comfortable chairs and a noticeboard with local and nursery activities displayed on it. There were comfortable chairs and room to leave buggies there while parents went to the classrooms.

The parents noticed that the nursery had a wide range of children from different cultures and backgrounds and that this was reflected in the toys, books, activities and displays in the nursery. Jane and Philip were very impressed and decided to put Davey's name down for a place at Minton Street.

Consider the case study and try and think about the reasons why Jane and Philip might have chosen Minton Street as a good option for their child. Why might a warm welcome be important to this couple in terms of their concerns about their child? There are some sample answers in the Appendix.

Good Communication and Information Sharing

The habit of exchanging information about the child and her circumstances should be established from the start of the relationship and continue on a daily basis.

Part of the greeting between the worker and the parent and the child might be a genuine enquiry about what the child has been doing. There is no formula to follow, except to have a joint interest in the child's well being and progress.

(Whalley 1997: 46)

You need to make time for communication both formally and informally, to ensure that parents are listened to and made to feel that their information is welcome. This may lead to occasions when you feel that parents are taking up your time discussing very minor issues, which seem trivial to you. However, by allowing parents to talk about their anxieties, you help them to reduce these and to build confidence in the care that their child is receiving. You also ensure that parents are able to discuss deeper concerns about their child with you if these arise. Developing communication skills is probably the single most crucial aspect of working with parents.

Draper and Duffy (2001) describe how differences in opinion about what is 'good for children' can be resolved through open, honest communication. In their example, parents recently arrived from Albania were leaving their children at the door of the crèche and refusing to come in and spend time with their children. Discussion revealed that in their home country this had been the norm and that the parents believed that leaving the children was best practice. This discussion paved the way to resolving the conflict that was developing between the crèche workers and parents.

A Chance to Think

Communication is essentially a two-way process of sending and receiving messages. We use speech to convey many of these messages, but much more information is contained in non-verbal communications. For example, you may be saying that it is fine for a parent to stop and talk to you for a few minutes, but if you are looking distracted, turning away, doing something else or talking to others at the same time, the message you are sending is clearly that you have not got time. Communication barriers may also arise through cultural differences or lack of information about the child and his family.

Exercise 5

Read the short scenarios below and for each, write notes on how the parent might feel and how communication could be improved. What underlying factors may be influencing the parent's behaviour at this time? How might the lack of effective communication disadvantage the child? It may help to check back to the underlying principles of partnership with parents at the beginning of this section of the chapter. Compare your answers with the sample answers in the Appendix.

SAM

Sam has been bringing his 3½-year-old daughter to the school nursery for six months. He seems very anxious that she should be learning reading and writing skills, and clearly does not feel that the staff 'push' her enough. The staff feel they have explained their position several times, but that Sam does not listen. Sam approaches a nursery nurse with a handful of workbooks on learning to read that he has bought. As he starts to tell the staff member about them, one of the other staff rolls her eyes up at the worker in sympathy and she smiles back. She then tells Sam that she is busy and has no time to talk to him.

ANJIE

Anjie arrives late again, bringing her 4-year-old son to be childminded while she is at work. As usual he looks half-asleep and half-dressed and the childminder knows he will not have had breakfast or a wash. She thinks Anjie should get the family up and ready earlier. She knows from local gossip that the other three children in the family are always late for school. The childminder greets Anjie without a smile, takes the child straight in and sighs with exasperation before the mother is out of earshot.

YASMIN

Yasmin and her mum come to playgroup for the fourth week running. Yasmin's mum does not talk to anyone and sits in the corner by herself. She wears a scarf over her head and a long dress, which covers her from top to toe. Last week some of the other parents were asking where she was from and whether she spoke English at all. Yasmin plays by herself and the other children ignore her.

PETER

Peter's mum picks him up late from after-school club for the third time running. A staff member is waiting at the door with him and he is handed over without a word. Later the staff member asks one of the management committee to ring her and tell her that late collection is unacceptable. Peter told the staff member that his mum has got a new job recently.

Communication Skills

The communication skills that are needed to work with parents are in some ways very similar to those needed for working with children. They include the following:

- listening attentively and encouraging parents to talk to you by using positive non-verbal skills such as smiling, making eye contact, avoiding interrupting
- seeking access to an interpreter if you and the parents do not have a language in common
- avoiding jargon
- sharing any concerns about the child in a non-accusatory way and listening and responding to parents' concerns
- suggesting the introduction of new practices as part of a partnership such as in dealing with difficult behaviour
- asking parents for advice and sharing their child-rearing practices

- taking a genuine interest in the child and parent
- asking parents for feedback on activities, resources and equipment in the setting
- taking time with parents
- giving praise to the child and parent
- giving information about the child in a positive manner
- being open and honest, but also tactful
- encouraging parents to look at the child's work and activities and become familiar with and comfortable in the setting.

Taking time to communicate at this level with parents may not seem too easy. However, the benefits of doing so are such that it is worthwhile considering how you can make more time for parents and encourage them to feel welcome in your setting.

Written communication with parents

Some information may be communicated in writing to parents. Early years centres often have brochures to give basic information about the centre and to outline policies such as equal opportunities or disability. Noticeboards at playgroups, nurseries and schools may have information about activities in the centre and local community. Nurseries and schools often send home information about forthcoming events on slips of paper. Parents may get information about their child's achievements and progress in writing. Other carers are less likely to communicate in writing, although foster carers and childminders sometimes keep written records about specific aspects of the child's development.

There are some limitations to written communication with parents. Not all parents may be able to read or understand the language used or they may not have sufficient literacy skills to decipher the contents of written communications. Written communications about individual children may contain important information, for example 'bump notes', reports of incidents or causes for concern about the child, so it is important to know that the parent is able to read this information before it is sent. Similarly, if you are in a setting where information about the child's progress is shared in writing, it is important to discuss this with parents so that they have an opportunity to go over the information and check their understanding of what is being conveyed. It is important when writing any communication for parents that you focus on simplicity, clarity and a friendly, positive tone. If the parent does not have English as a first language, it is important to ensure that a translation is available or that other means of communication are used.

 A Chance to Think

Sometimes there are barriers to good communication with parents. These might include class and cultural differences, language differences, physical disabilities such as speech, hearing or sight impairment or simply a gap in your understanding of good early years practices. Barriers to communication may also exist because it is hard to access the setting or because the routines and structure of the day do not give you time for a chat at picking-up or dropping-off times. Some parents may feel shy about approaching you or worry about taking up your time.

Exercise 6

Think about parents you work with and identify a few with whom the communication has not been as good as it could have been. For each, make a note of the barriers to communication that prevented a better level of contact. Consider the parent, yourself and the setting. Bear in mind any cultural differences or feelings you might have had about the parents which could have influenced the quality of communication with them. Then note ways that the communication could have been improved and how you might have started to achieve better relationships with these parents.

Sharing Responsibility and Accountability

This involves ensuring that you and the parents are working as a team to provide the best standard of care you can for the child. The child's welfare has to come first and in order to ensure this, you and the parents need to work towards a common view of what you are trying to achieve with the child. To do this, you need to establish a position from the start of the relationship with the parent, that you respect their views, believe they have the child's best interests at heart and want the best for their child. (It may be helpful to check back to the list of underlying principles of partnership with parents at the beginning of this section of the chapter.)

Parents who are struggling to cope need support, not criticism. If parents feel that they are respected and valued as experts on their own children, then they may be more open to listening to your suggestions for improving the child's experience and they may be able to share the problems they have encountered in trying to achieve these improvements. It is important to remember that there are many different successful parenting styles and not all of these will be familiar to all early years workers.

Think *A Chance to Think*

One of the most difficult circumstances you may encounter in working towards partnership with parents and others is when you fundamentally disagree with the style and quality of the childcare that others, perhaps parents, provide.

Finding a way of communicating your concerns without causing resentments or conflict can be a delicate task requiring a great deal of tact. Good communication, emphasizing the positive and offering help to effect change can be a useful way to proceed. Criticizing, offering unwanted advice and implying that parents are failing the child will not work to improve the child's condition and may result in a worse state of affairs.

Exercise 7

Read the case study and answer the questions. You may find it helpful to discuss your answers with a colleague or friend and check them with the sample answers in the Appendix.

CHANTELLE

Chantelle has been coming to you to be childminded for about two or three months as part of a support package arranged by social services. You understand that there have been concerns about Chantelle's care and the lack of good supervision in the home. Chantelle is 3 and she lives with her mother and three older brothers. She has settled down well with you and has started to respond to your efforts to involve her in play and activities.

You have become increasingly concerned about the level of supervision in the home. Chantelle has told you that she is left in the care of her 9-year-old brother and she does not like this because her brothers fight when her mother is out. She plays out on the street on her own at home and does not understand why she is not allowed to do this at your house. Recently the mother sent the 9-year-old brother to collect Chantelle and when you refused to send her home with him, the mother collected Chantelle in a very angry mood.

1 What issues do you think this case study raises about Chantelle's care that need to be addressed?
2 How would you start to approach these issues and who would need to be involved in this process?
3 What sort of communication skills would you need in order to ensure that the outcomes of any discussions are positive?
4 What sort of support might you offer the mother in order to improve circumstances for Chantelle?

It is always important to convey your values and standards to the parent in an honest and straightforward manner, especially if they conflict with the parents' views. If you are able to do this without implying criticism of the parent you may be able to reach a better understanding and more positive relationship.

Cultural differences can have a major impact on the care of the child. Most parents take for granted that their cultural rituals will be respected in the childcare setting. For example, that birthdays and Christmas will be celebrated, that children will eat familiar food and play games that parents can understand the purpose of, and that the child will be surrounded by familiar images and customs. If the child is from a minority culture this simply may not be the case. In order to take on some of the responsibility for nurturing the child's sense of her own culture, it may be necessary to ask the parents about their customs and practices. Admitting that you do not have this information may be difficult at first, but parents may be very pleased that you have asked them about their lives and they will probably be glad to help. In this way you can introduce images and customs into the setting which are familiar to the child and which may be of great interest to other children, parents and staff.

Most early years training involves exploring how to support children in their different cultures. However, it is important to remember not to assume that a family has particular customs and beliefs because of their name or external appearance. It is also important to remember that supporting children in their culture involves talking to the child and family about the practices and beliefs that they value and respecting these in the same way as you would your own.

Difficulties in Creating Partnerships with Parents

Some of the barriers to working in partnership with parents have already been discussed, for example communication difficulties, cultural differences, busy staff, lack of appreciation of the contributions that parents can make. However, there are some specific circumstances in which forming partnerships with parents may be particularly hard. If a child has been subject to child protection procedures and parents have placed their child in the setting as part of a child protection plan, the parent may well not have chosen the setting themselves and this may result in resentments or the parent not wanting to get involved. If parents are under stress they may be angry or unhappy with you as part of the expression of that stress.

You cannot instantly remove barriers to creating and maintaining partnerships. However, by remaining courteous and supportive, by continuing to take an interest in the child and family and encouraging parents to talk to you about their child you may well improve the relationship to the benefit of all concerned. Read through the case studies in Exercises 3, 4, 5, 7 and 'Jenny' again and remind yourself of the importance of not judging parents, but instead trying to support them in the often difficult task of parenting their children.

Conclusions

Working with parents can be difficult at times, particularly if they are harder to reach or they have differing views from you about acceptable standards of childcare practice. However, working together is crucial to support the child's best interests and can be of great benefit to the parents and childcare workers as well.

Working with Other Professionals

Early years workers may have to work in partnership with other professionals for a number of different reasons depending on job role. Foster carers and family centre workers will probably have regular contact with social workers. Nurseries will have varying degrees of contact with school staff, social workers and others. Everybody has contact with OFSTED inspectors. All early years workers could come into contact with a wide range of other professionals through, for example, child protection investigations or to support a child with learning or behavioural difficulties.

Working with other agencies can be stressful if it is unclear what is expected of you in partnership or where the expectations of your role seem to conflict with those of other professionals involved with the child. However, as with working with parents, the best interests of the child can be met only through the harmonious and coordinated efforts of the various workers involved.

Failure to 'work together' can have tragic consequences for children and families and sometimes practitioners. The Laming Report (2003) on the findings of the inquiry into Victoria Climbie's death at the hands of her aunt and her aunt's boyfriend concluded that failures of agencies to work together and share information had been significant in the circumstances leading to Victoria's death. Almost every other child death inquiry report through the 1980s and 1990s has drawn similar conclusions. Working in partnership between professionals and agencies is identified as a key professional role in the Children Act 1989, in the child protection guidelines 'Working Together to Safeguard Children' (DoH, 1999) and in all key documents relating to current work with children and families including early years care and education services. Recently, in response to the failures identified by Lord Laming in Victoria Climbie's case (Laming, 2003), the Green Paper 'Every Child Matters' (DfES, 2003) outlines proposals to increasingly integrate different aspects of children's services in order to ensure increased professional cooperation.

In order to achieve good working relationships with other agency staff there are a number of questions to consider:

- Do you understand the agency/job role of others involved?
- Do you know why they are involved with the child and what goals they are working towards with the child and family?

- Do these goals match or conflict with your goals for the child?
- Are you responsible for monitoring any aspect of the child's condition or behaviour?
- Are you responsible for reporting any progress or concerns to another agency?
- Are the parents aware of your role in relation to other professionals and if not, why not?
- What mechanisms do you have for communicating with the other agencies involved with a child and are they effective?

Perhaps the single most important feature of good working partnerships is effective communication systems. Lack of communication can lead to families failing to receive all the support they need or being swamped with too many professionals. Taylor (1998, p. 293) suggest that 'Case conferencing is one of the better ways of ensuring that each professional group is aware of its boundaries and responsibilities when more than one group is involved in the care of the child'.

A Chance to Think

It can take time to establish good working relationships with other professionals and to recognize their role in respect of the child and family. Reflecting back on the types of partnerships you have had with others in the past can be very positive in achieving a better understanding of how to establish and maintain 'working together' relationships in the future.

Exercise 8

1 Think about any contact you may have had with workers from other agencies in respect of different children in your care. Look at the questions on pp. 144–5 and answer them with reference to one or more children. Write down any problems that you had working with others and how you might tackle these in future.
2 Read the case study and answer the questions. Discuss your answers with a colleague or friend.

WILLIAM

William (aged 2) is coming to nursery as part of a support plan for his family. His mother has two other children and is suffering from depression, which has resulted at times in unacceptably low standards of childcare. William's mother, Stella, finds him particularly difficult to cope with. The social worker came to see you and talked about the family in positive terms, emphasizing that the plan was to maintain the family as a unit and support Stella to be a better parent. He talked to you about the areas of family life which were working well and those which the family needed help with. He told you about some of the other support the family was getting. He answered your questions fully and clearly, but he did not tell you about some areas of Stella's background, as these were confidential.

When you met William's mother you already had positive feelings about her and some sympathy for her difficulties. You welcomed her warmly and settled down to talk to her about William and the sort of care you could offer him. You asked her advice on several areas of care, including eating and controlling his sometimes difficult behaviour. Stella was initially reluctant but she opened up after a while and talked about William and the problems she was having with him. You were able to remind her of the areas where things were going well and to offer your support. At the end of the meeting Stella told you she was very happy William was coming to you and that she was glad you were a nice person.

1 In what way did the discussion with the social worker influence the first meeting with Stella?
2 How might this benefit William, Stella and you?
3 What sort of contact would you expect to have with the social worker and how do you see his role?

REFERENCES AND FURTHER READING

Athey, C. (1990) *Extending Thought in Young Children*. London: Paul Chapman.

Bastiani, J. (1995) *Taking a Few Risks*. London: Royal Society for the Encouragement of Arts, Manufacture & Commerce.

Beaver, M., Brewster, J., Jones, P., Keene, A., Neaum, S. and Tallock, J. (1999) *Babies and Young Children Book 2: Early Years Care and Education* (2nd edn). Cheltenham: Stanley Thornes.

Department of Education and Science (DfES) (1990) *Starting with Quality: Report of the Committee of Inquiry into the Educational Experience offered to Three and Four Year Olds* (Rumbold Report). London: HMSO.

DfES (2001) 'National Standards for Under Eight's Daycare and Childminding.'

DfES (2001) 'Special Educational Needs Code of Practice.' www.dfes.gov.uk

DfES (2003) 'Every Child Matters.' www.dfes.gov.uk/everychildmatters

Department of Health (DoH) (1999) 'Working Together to Safeguard Children.'

Draper, L. and Duthy, B. 'Working with Parents', in G. Pugh, (2001) *Contemporary Issues in the Early Years: Working Collaboratively for Children* (3rd edn). London: Paul Chapman, in association with the National Children's Bureau.

Department of Health (1999) *Working Together to Safeguard Children*. London: HMSO.

Hobart, C. and Frankel, J. (1999) *Childminding: A Guide to Good Practice*. Cheltenham: Stanley Thornes.

Lindon, J. and Lindon, L. (1993) *Caring for the Under-8's: Working to Achieve Good Practice*. London: Macmillan.

Pugh, G., De'Ath, E. and Smith, C. (1994) *Confident Parents: Confident Children: Policy and Practice in Parent Education and Support*. London: National Children's Bureau.

QCA (2000) 'Curriculum Guidance for the Foundation Stage.'

Sure Start (2002) 'Birth to Three Matters.' www.surestart.org.uk

Tassoni, P. (1998) *Child Care and Education*. Oxford: Heinemann.

Tassoni, P., Beith, K., Eldridge, H. and Gough, A. (1999) *Nursery Nursing: A Guide to Work in Early Years*. Oxford: Heinemann.

Taylor, J. (1998) 'Working with Young Children and Their Families', in J. Taylor and M. Woods (eds) *Early Childhood Studies: An Holistic Introduction*. London: Arnold.

Woods, M. (1998) 'Early Childhood Education in Pre-school Settings', in J. Taylor and M. Woods (eds) *Early Childhood Studies: An Holistic Introduction*. London: Arnold.

Victoria Climbie Inquiry – Report of an Inquiry by Lord Laming (January 2003). London: The Stationery Office. www.victoria-climbie-inquiry.org.uk

Whalley, M. (1997) *Working with Parents*. London: Hodder and Stoughton.

8

Confidentiality

INTRODUCTION

The concept of confidentiality is central to good practice in childcare and early years education, and every textbook on caring for children has a section on the need to maintain confidentiality. Despite this, confidentiality is a good practice issue that is sometimes ignored by workers and managers alike. While some information about children and their families is kept confidential by all concerned, other information is sometimes widely discussed and occasionally gossiped about.

Confidentiality is important because it is a basis to building trusting, cooperative working relationships with parents and other workers. Maintaining confidentiality is an important part of developing good standards of professionalism. However, being able to recognize the difference between information that needs to be kept confidential and information that does not can be complex at times. In addition, there are some circumstances in which confidentiality may have to be broken in order to serve the best interests of the child. This can lead to dilemmas about whether to break confidentiality or not in particular circumstances.

> *All parents must be able to feel confident that their lives will not be fuel for gossip. This includes conversations between you and other staff as well as those with parents. However, you need to be honest in your first contact with parents about the circumstances under which you could not promise to keep a secret: events that could affect a child's well-being or safety would have to be passed on to colleagues or your senior.*
>
> (Lindon and Lindon 1993: 27)

In this chapter we will look at the types of information that early years workers may gather and record about children and their families and how to keep this information confidential. Many settings have confidentiality policies or guidelines that are the basis of good practice, and these often include the concept of 'need to know' when sharing information with others. Confidentiality is also usually part of national guidelines or statements of good practice such as the CACHE 'Statement of Values' issued to all CACHE-registered students (Tassoni *et al.*, 1999).

The chapter also explores the difficult issue of deciding when it is necessary to break confidentiality. Early years workers may sometimes find themselves in situations where there is much uncertainty about when and how information should be passed on. The outcomes of passing on information inappropriately will be explored, as will good practice in record-keeping and storing.

The Concept of Confidentiality

Confidentiality is a concept that has become more significant in all areas of care in recent years. In early years practice, confidentiality has become central to the codes of good practice in all settings and in relation to all job roles. The concept of confidentiality in the early years is based on the rights of children and families to anti-discriminatory practice and their rights to respect and support from early years workers. As much of good quality early years work is based on partnership with parents, they need to have confidence that personal, and sometimes sensitive, information about themselves and their child will be kept safely and transferred to the absolute minimum numbers of other workers.

If you consider the world we live in at present, there is an astonishing number of ways in which information about individuals and families is gathered and stored. Some of this information is for important purposes such as medical records and basic identification data (birth records, for example). Other information is kept for marketing purposes or to check on financial status (such as credit referencing information). A lot of information is stored and used without our explicit knowledge and permission. As mass communications continue to develop at a rapid pace, increasing amounts of information about individuals and families are available on an ever-increasing scale.

Despite this, there is a lot of personal information that we would all prefer to keep to ourselves. Information about family relationships, medical conditions, family crises, breakdowns or rifts may all come into this category. Such information may influence how others see us or relate to us. In some circumstances such information may affect our place in the community and our level of acceptance by friends and acquaintances.

 A Chance to Think

Individuals share information about themselves to varying degrees. Whereas some people seem to discuss many things about themselves openly with a wide range of others, there are others who do not share personal information with anyone. Most of us fall between these extremes. We may share quite a lot of information about ourselves but there may be other events or facts that we do not want the majority of others to know about for a variety of reasons.

 Exercise 1

Think about yourself and possibly your family. Try to make a note of several pieces of information about you that you would not wish to share with others or that you have shared with only a very few people. Some of this information may still be quite painful or may raise issues that you have not thought about for some time. Consider how it might make you feel if this information was passed on to friends, work colleagues and neighbours. Would you be happy about this? How do you think it may affect how others see you if they had this information? Might it affect your own view of yourself if others had this information about you? Summarize the value to you of keeping this information confidential.

The concept of confidentiality is a difficult one to grasp at times. In order to provide a high standard of care and education to the children, there is a lot of information about the child and family which early years workers need to know. In some cases, for example, where the child has a potentially life-threatening medical condition, it is absolutely crucial to have information about this. However, in order to balance confidentiality and the need to have certain information in order to provide good standards of care, it is important to think carefully about the different types of information gathered and stored on children and their families, and to consider what is confidential and what is not.

Changes in the ways information can be shared between agencies may be on their way. The Green Paper 'Every Child Matters' (DfES, 2003) proposes changes to current confidentiality requirements to facilitate sharing of information between agencies to better protect children from abuse. This may lead to a considerable level of debate about confidentiality versus information-sharing as concerns about human rights and the invasion of privacy contend with the need to share information as part of child protection processes.

Confidentiality in Early Years Care and Education

Gathering Information about the Child and Family

Perhaps one of the simplest rules of gathering information about other people is the 'need-to-know' basis. For example, if you are stopped by a market researcher while out shopping, apparently to discuss your views on chocolate or shampoo, you may find yourself answering a series of questions which include your age, marital status, income bracket and so on. The question you may ask yourself is whether this information is really needed or not. Sometimes information is gathered that appears to have no real purpose in terms of the current task. It may be gathered for other purposes without the knowledge or permission of the provider. On the other hand it may be useful for the present task in ways that are not obvious. The important point is to try to develop a critical view of the process of gathering information about children and families in the work setting. Is the information being gathered really needed, and if so, what is it needed for? How sensitive is the information? Do normal confidentiality precautions apply or should certain information be kept very confidential?

A Chance to Think

Parents usually have to fill at least one form in to provide information about the child and themselves, whatever the early years setting. This information is kept on record to be used as required. All information gathered about the child and her family should have a purpose that is relevant to the needs of the child within the setting. In order to ensure that the right type of information is gathered, forms should be reviewed regularly to make sure they gather relevant information only.

Exercise 2

Obtain copies of the records you keep in the workplace or placement. Look at the information they gather and make a note of the purposes that this information has that are relevant to the setting. For example, telephone numbers of a range of family members and friends may be kept, in order to be able to find a responsible adult in an emergency. If there is any information request that you do not understand the purpose of, ask your supervisor or the person in charge.

Who 'Needs to Know?'

When considering access to information about the child and her family it is important to think of 'who needs to know?' Information should be available only to early years workers and others who need it in order to offer the child and family a good quality service. In the vast majority of cases, information requests from outside the setting should be met only with the parent's agreement.

Even basic information such as names, addresses, telephone numbers and emergency contacts should be kept in a safe place and have restricted access. There may be good reasons why parents do not want their names and addresses to be generally available. For example, if a woman has been subject to domestic violence by her male partner, she may have been rehoused away from the area they lived in, for her own safety. It may be risking her safety if information about her whereabouts is easily accessed. Professional staff within the setting will have access to basic information about children and their families, but access may be witheld from students on placement. Other agencies may need to have some information. The process of transferring information outside the setting while maintaining confidentiality will be explored later in the chapter.

More sensitive information may need to be available only to a small number of staff. For example, in a school setting this might be the head and class teacher. In a nursery, it may be the person in charge and the key worker or group leader. Obviously, in a single carer setting, all information is held by one person, but that carer may share information more often with other agencies such as social services.

Sensitive information may include the following:

- details of mental or physical illnesses suffered by the parent
- details of any illnesses or impairments the child may have
- child protection issues or investigations that have arisen in respect of any child in the family
- family conflict, domestic violence
- separation, divorce, details of contact arrangements for the child
- restricted child–parent contact, for example where a court order exists that restrains a parent from contact with the child or limits that contact
- details of the child's legal status in the family such as adopted children, stepchildren, foster children
- location of parents, for example where a parent has deserted the family or is in prison.

Not all of this information may have been gathered formally or recorded. Some of this type of information may be known only because parents have passed it on to the early years worker. They may have given the information because they thought it might help with the worker's understanding of the child's needs or to explain some of the apparent stresses or strains within the family. The parent may also have shared sensitive information with the worker because they needed a good listener and felt that the worker might offer support and understanding.

The early years worker may record sensitive information if it is directly relevant to the care of the child. If it is not, it may be better to remain aware of the information but not to record it. If the worker feels unsure of whether to record information about the family or not, it is helpful to ask the supervisor's advice. Parents should be aware that information might be kept in confidential records and should have access to the information kept about their child.

Think | A Chance to Think

Deciding whether to pass information to others in the setting (or in the case of single carer settings, to support workers) can be a difficult judgement to make at times. Parents may have talked to the early years worker about some aspect of their lives in confidence and might be appalled to think that this information may be recorded and discussed with others. However, failing to pass on information about some aspect of the child's health or welfare which has an impact on the child's behaviour and/or condition might seriously affect the quality of care the child receives. Many early years settings or roles have confidentiality policies to reassure parents and remind workers of their responsibilities. These can be useful guidelines when you are unsure about confidentiality in particular situations.

Exercise 3

Read the following short scenarios and decide in each case who would need to know the information, apart from you. Bear in mind that parents would need to be aware that the information has been passed on in order to best meet the child's interests. Would you pass the information on verbally and record it? Check any confidentiality policy relevant to your setting or job role for guidelines. Compare your answers with the sample answers in the Appendix.

ELLY

Elly is 5. She is in reception class at school and you are the teaching assistant. Her father came to speak to you about a hearing test Elly had had the week before, which implied that Elly's hearing was impaired in one ear. Further tests are planned. Elly's father was concerned that she should not struggle at school in the meanwhile, but related at length his concerns that she might be stigmatized if the information was widely known.

MARK

Mark is 4. His mother has looked dreadfully tired and down for the last few weeks and when you enquired after her health she confided that she was depressed and had visited her doctor for help. Mark's mother is a single parent with few supports. You work at the nursery Mark has attended for over a year. You have noticed that he seems a bit subdued at present.

ROSE AND DAISY

Rose and Daisy are 2-year-old twins. You have childminded them for a year as both parents work. Their father rang this morning to tell you he would be late. When he arrived he collapsed in floods of tears, telling you that his wife had left him to live with another man and that she intended to take the twins as soon as she had found a place for them to live.

FRANK AND DEAN

Frank (6) and Dean (8) come to the after-school club where you work. Their mother took you aside recently to tell you that the boys' father had threatened to snatch them from her care and she showed you a court order confirming that he was not to have contact with them. You know that the boys' father has been very violent to all the family in the past.

Breaking Confidences

It may be helpful at this stage to consider some of the consequences of breaking confidences inappropriately. One of the problems with confidentiality in this area is that, like many caring jobs, early years practice can be stressful, and emotionally and physically exhausting. There can also be upsetting experiences in some settings, especially for early years workers who work with children in distress. It can feel natural to want to share experiences with colleagues, family members and friends in order to unwind and 'off-load' some of the stress. It is also difficult sometimes to pinpoint when a general conversation with a parent or parents becomes a gossip about another parent or even another staff member. The majority of breaches of confidence are probably not malicious, but are thoughtless and unconsidered. We can all be susceptible to the desire to be the one with the exciting news!

Think · A Chance to Think

The consequences of breaking confidences should be carefully considered in order to better understand the need for good practice in this area.

Exercise 4

Read the short scenarios below and consider the outcomes of the breach of confidentiality in terms of the child, the parent, you and the setting.

LUCY

Lucy's mother Paula, who is 40, has told you in confidence that she is expecting another baby, but that she does not want to tell many people until she has had tests for foetal abnormality. You tell another parent in strictest confidence, but word gets round, and eventually a parent congratulates Paula on her good news.

PAUL

Paul is currently staying with foster carers because he is the subject of a child protection investigation. Another parent comments on a stranger dropping him off in the morning and a colleague tells him that Paul is in care, but that the reasons why are a secret.

BILLY

Billy's father Fred has been sentenced to six months in prison. His mother told you in strictest confidence. However, at a meeting a colleague asks you if it is true and tells you that all the parents are gossiping about Billy's family. Apparently, a parent overheard your partner telling a friend in the local shop.

A breach of confidentiality could lead to loss of confidence in the early years worker and possibly disciplinary action or dismissal, or for childminders, loss of earnings. At the very least, it would damage the trust between the worker, parent and child. 'Years of work in building good parent relationships can be put at risk if, through thoughtlessness or temptation, an early years worker repeats information to inappropriate people' (Tassoni 1998, p. 230).

In some circumstances it could have embarrassing or humiliating consequences for the child and family, possibly the unpleasantness of being gossiped about or perhaps being ostracized by others in the community. In other situations, the outcomes could be even more serious, as in the example of a family in hiding from a violent father. The setting, whether it is a nursery, childminder, school, pre-school or foster home, could lose credibility with parents and other agencies. It is possible that the child might be withdrawn from the setting, causing her distress due to the disruption. In situations where parents depend on their early years placement for support because they are struggling with the task of parenting, this could have serious consequences.

Finally, it is also important to remember that information passed surreptitiously from one person to another can lead to the 'Chinese Whispers' effect, where information becomes increasingly distorted until it is simply untrue. Avoiding breaches of confidence in the first place can ensure that this does not happen. Good practice should include:

- Be aware that all information is potentially confidential.
- Apply the 'needs-to-know' rule to passing on any information.
- Keep information to yourself if no one else in the setting needs to know.
- Talk to parents if you need to pass information on to colleagues.
- Explain to parents that information will be kept confidential except in circumstances where the child's well-being is at stake.
- Know the relevant policy and guidelines on confidentiality.
- Avoid discussions with parents about other parents.
- Discuss children and parents in professional terms with colleagues, avoiding criticizing them or making generalized statements about them.
- Be aware of the possible consequences of breaking confidentiality.

Deciding to Break Confidences – When and Why

Child Protection

Most of the time confidential information can remain confidential and does not need to be passed on outside the setting or even within the setting. However, there are a few situations where confidentiality may have to be broken in order to safeguard the child's best interests. The most common circumstance in which it is considered necessary to break confidentiality about children and their families is when a child protection issue arises. In this case the duty to protect the child outweighs considerations of confidentiality. The 'Principles of Excellence in Childminding Practice' developed by the National Childminding Association and CACHE sum this up as follows:

Information about children and families must never be shared with others, without the permission of the family, except in the interests of protecting children – for instance, in the case of suspected abuse. In the latter case, correct procedures must be followed, and information passes only to appropriate personnel or agencies as set out in such procedures.

(Hobart and Frankel 1999: 227)

If you suspect that abuse may have taken place, it is crucial that you take steps to protect the child, even if this means breaking confidentiality.

The Department of Health 1999 guidelines *Working Together to Safeguard Children* on inter-agency cooperation to protect children from abuse emphasize this point, stating that providers of information about children should always be aware that if child protection issues arise, information may not be kept confidential.

The prospect of dealing with such a situation may be daunting. If the child protection issue is a false alarm, it may be that angry parents withdraw their child from the setting. This could have serious consequences for the livelihoods of some early years workers. Childminders rely on their reputations to keep and attract children to their care. Nurseries in the independent sector may also rely on their positive relationships with parents to remain in business. However, protecting children must override these considerations in all cases. All early years workers have a responsibility to be aware of the potential for abuse and to respond to any suspicions that abuse has taken place.

In order to minimize the risk of damage to your relationship with the family and wider community, all discussions about suspected abuse should be kept strictly confidential and should be treated with the greatest sensitivity. Normally, if a referral is to be made to social services about suspected child abuse, parents should be informed unless this would put the child at greater risk.

Think) *A Chance to Think*

If you are faced with a potential child protection issue, it is important to consider carefully whether you would share your concerns, who you might share them with and how confidentiality can be maintained at this stage.

Exercise 5

Read the case study and answer the following questions. Ask a colleague to answer them too and compare and discuss your answers. You can also compare your answers with the sample answers in the Appendix.

KASSIM

Kassim is 6. You are the teaching assistant in his class at school. You noticed today that Kassim has some facial bruising and that he was reluctant to go outside at play. He sat alone in the yard, with his arms wrapped round his body. When you sat with him and spoke to him, he cried, but would not tell you what was wrong. You have been concerned about Kassim for a time. He is very subdued at times. His mother is often angry with him, shouting at him at home time for not getting his things together quickly enough, and criticizing him openly, calling him a 'stupid boy'. You have become aware that physical punishment is common within the family from the comments of Kassim's older sister. When she sees you with Kassim she approaches and tells you he is upset because he has been punished for being 'a very naughty boy'.

1 Describe any concerns you may have about Kassim.
2 Would you share these concerns with anyone, and if so, who would it be?
3 What steps would you take to minimize any breach of confidentiality at this stage?

Suspicions about child abuse

There are a number of steps to take if abuse is suspected. First, the early years worker should record concerns, possibly about a single incident, possibly over a period of time. This record should include any indicators of abuse, disclosure of abuse by the child, outcomes of discussions with parents and information from others. Any written notes should be kept in a safe place, inaccessible to others. Concerns or suspicions of abuse should be discussed in strictest confidence with an appropriate person. This could be the child protection liaison teacher in a school, a nursery head, the support worker for childminders and the support social worker for foster carers. In other settings, it may be a trusted colleague with experience and a high level of professionalism. It may be hard, particularly for childminders who work alone, not to share concerns with family members or friends, but this would be totally inappropriate.

If the other worker agrees that there are concerns about the child, then these must be passed to the local authority social services department. Many early years settings have internal procedures for handling suspected abuse, and all early years workers should be familiar with these. Details of the responsibilities of different early years workers are outlined in the area child protection procedures.

There should be a copy in every early years setting and the local library. Many voluntary and independent early years providers have agreements with social services about passing on concerns about possible abuse.

The resulting child protection investigation should be handled with the maximum level of confidentiality. It is important that during the investigation the early years worker does not talk to any other staff or parents about the concerns that are being investigated. This may be quite difficult, especially if the early years worker is anxious about the outcomes of the investigation and concerned about the child. However, it is important to share worries only with a supervisor, who may be able to listen and offer support.

In some cases, the child may be on the Child Protection Register prior to being placed in the early years setting. This information may be part of the information given to the early years worker at the time of placement, for example where a social worker seeks a placement as part of the child protection plan. In these cases the early years workers may have a role in monitoring the child's progress and condition which has been discussed and agreed with the social worker or at the child protection case conference. The parent should be aware that early years workers have this role and that they may pass information to the social worker or review case conference as part of this role. Good practice in child protection should ensure that parents are informed of all concerns about their child.

If you are not sure about any aspect of child protection, discuss this with your supervisor or support worker and ask if training is available. Child protection references can be found at the end of the chapter.

Other Circumstances

There are a number of other circumstances in which it may be necessary to compromise confidentiality of information about children and their families. For example, if a child is suffering from a communicable illness such as chicken pox, or an infestation such as head lice, then it is necessary to warn other parents that their children may contract the illness or infestation. Although it is normal good practice to inform other parents without identifying the carrier, it is often obvious who the child is, especially in settings where there are few children. In most cases, this causes little distress as the majority of parents accept childhood illnesses and minor infestations as part of parenting. However, it is good practice to let parents know that others have to be informed without directly naming their child.

It may not be obvious whether information about a child's medical condition should be shared with other workers and parents or not. It is helpful to discuss the purpose of sharing the information with the parent and to seek their permission to pass it on. If this is not possible, but you believe the welfare of the child or other children may be compromised if you do not pass on information, talk to your supervisor in confidence and/or check any available guidelines or policies. The consequences of passing on information about medical conditions should be considered very carefully before confidentiality is breached.

Exercise 6

Read the case study below and answer the questions. Sample answers are in the Appendix. You may like to read about HIV in children or check the information in the sample answers if this is an area you are not familiar with.

CATHY

Cathy is 8. She is about to be placed with you for fostering because her mother is ill and cannot care for her. Other family members have refused to care for her because of her HIV positive status. The social worker has discussed the implications of Cathy's HIV infection with you at length. From these discussions, put a tick against anyone you agree needs to know about Cathy's infection:

- doctor
- teacher/school
- dentist
- your extended family
- neighbours
- playmates' parents
- your children.

Explain why you would pass on the information in each case and how revealing this information may affect Cathy and/or you and your family.

Good Practice Guidelines

Not all circumstances in which confidentiality might have to be breached can be listed here. However, there are some general good practice guidelines which should be considered if a situation arises in which it is unclear whether or nor confidences need to be broken:

- Will maintaining confidentiality or breaking confidentiality best serve the child's interests?
- Is there a legal or policy issue involved, for example if confidential information is required as part of a police investigation?
- Can the issue be discussed with parents and their permission to disclose information sought?
- Have you discussed the situation in confidence with a senior colleague?
- Are there any relevant workplace or job role guidelines or policies which could help you to make a decision?

Record-Keeping and Storage of Information

Protecting and Sharing Written Information

In any early years setting there will be some written information about the child and the family. Although the quantity of information may vary between settings, in all cases this information needs to be kept safely and access to it restricted. This means that information should not be accessible to other parents or to colleagues who do not have a need to know. It is a good policy to ensure that parents are aware of any written records about their own child and family and to give them access to the information. Records should be checked for accuracy with the parent and any inaccuracies altered immediately. Information may be paper-based or on a computer database. In both cases it is important to ensure that the place the information is kept in is away from others and can be locked. The Data Protection Act 1984 requires anyone keeping personal data on a computer to register with the Data Protection Register. Information can be requested by individuals who have the right to make corrections if this turns out to be inaccurate.

Childminders and foster carers who keep records in their own home need to ensure that other family members do not have access to these. In other settings, it is important to ensure that people cannot easily gain access to filing cabinets or computer databases. One example of poor practice was a doctor's surgery where the patient was asked to take a seat in the consulting room and had the opportunity to read the previous patient's notes on the monitor while the doctor talked to the nurse outside.

Think *A Chance to Think*

In all settings, thought should be given to how written information can be stored safely, checked for inaccuracies and shared with parents.

162

Think about the written information you keep on parents or which is kept at your work site or placement. How is it stored? Is it accessible to other parents, colleagues who do not need to know, or visitors? How is information updated or amended? Are systems for checking the accuracy of data with parents in place? Why might it be important to ensure that data is accurate, up-to-date and confidential? Discuss your answers with a colleague or supervisor.

Sharing Information with Colleagues from Other Agencies

Sometimes colleagues from other agencies may ask for existing information about a child or family, or ask that new information about the child be gathered on their behalf, for example through observations or assessments. In order to ensure that this information is kept confidential it is important that in the majority of cases the child's parents are in agreement with the plan to share existing information or gather new information about the child. Much of this exchange of information will be done with colleagues who are helping the child with specific areas of development or difficulty, such as speech therapists, educational psychologists or health visitors. In these cases it is usual that parents are in agreement with the plans to share information and that the information is shared with the parents as well.

In some child protection situations, the early years worker may be gathering and/or sharing information as part of a child protection plan for a child who is on the Child Protection Register. Normally parents will be aware of this and have access to the information, as social workers try to work in partnership with parents. However, in a minority of cases this sort of partnership may not be possible and parents may not be given access to the information. It is very important to check whether parents are aware of information gathering and sharing as regards their child and to be sure that the requirements of the situation are clear to all involved.

When sharing information with other agencies, it is important to be clear that:

- It has been decided that the information should be shared between the setting and the other agency, normally with the parent's agreement.
- The type and range of information to be shared is clear.
- The information is passed only to other agency staff who need to know.
- Written information is passed in sealed envelopes and is kept confidentially.
- The identity of callers on the phone is checked before information is passed.

The basic rule of thumb is to share no information unless you are sure this is the right course of action and to check with appropriate others if in doubt.

Observation and Assessment

Information gathered during observation and assessment of children needs to be kept confidential in the same way as other information about the child. 'As you observe and record children's behaviour in your observations, you may discover and identify information concerning the child or her family. Never record anything you would be unwilling to share with parents' (Hobart and Frankel 1999, p. 183). Take particular care to make sure that notes are destroyed once the observation is written up and that observations are shared only with parents and colleagues who need to know. It is necessary to gain the parent's agreement to observations in the first place and to ensure that the parent knows the purpose of the observation or assessment and whom the information will be shared with.

There are particular requirements when students on placement are doing observations as part of their studies. Observations are an important part of childcare education and training, but they involve gathering a lot of information about children that must be handled carefully. Good practice guidelines for students doing observations include the following:

- The student should be fully aware of the confidentiality policy of the early years setting or role.
- Students should always have permission to do observations.
- The student should be clear about who can share the observation information and who cannot.
- The observation notes and final write-ups should be anonymous from the start, for example changing the child's name, using age and not date of birth, describing the setting but not naming it, avoiding naming any staff.
- Records should be kept in a safe place and transported safely.
- Supervisors should check that students are keeping information safely and that they are maintaining confidentiality.
- Students should be careful not to use real names and other identifying information when discussing children in college.

An example of breach of confidentiality in this area involved a student on a college childcare and education course. During a college class on child protection, the student raised some concerns about a child he had been observing. Before the tutor could prevent him, he named the child, having already identified the setting. Two of the other students in the class knew the child and his family.

Students need to be particularly careful about transporting observation notes and assessment sheets between the placement, college and home. Supervisors have a role in emphasizing to students the importance of confidentiality in making and keeping records.

Conclusions

Confidentiality of information is a key feature of good practice in early years care and education. Many breaches of confidentiality happen because of thoughtlessness or lack of understanding of the possible consequences. In some cases, unfortunately, lack of confidentiality is part of the worksite culture. However, to establish effective working relationships with parents and others, early years workers must be trustworthy and reliable. Confidentiality is central to this process of building trusting relationships and to the concept of professionalism in early years care and education. Confidential information should never be passed on without either the parent's agreement or because it has been decided that in order to safeguard the child's best interests, confidentiality must be broken.

REFERENCES AND FURTHER READING

Area child protection procedures (available from the local library or in the workplace).

Department of Health (DoH) (1999) *Working Together to Safeguard Children*. London: HMSO.

Hobart, C. and Frankel, J. (1999) *Childminding: A Guide to Good Practice*. Cheltenham: Stanley Thorne.

Kay, J. (2003) *Protecting Children* (2nd edn). London: Continuum.

Lindon, J. and Lindon, L. (1993) *Caring for the Under-8s: Working to Achieve Good Practice.* London: Macmillan.

O'Hagan, M. (1997) *Geraghty's Caring for Children* (3rd edn). London: Ballière Tindall.

Tassoni, P. (1998) *Child Care and Education*. Oxford: Heinemann.

Tassoni, P., Beith, K., Eldridge, H. and Gough, A. (1999) *Nursery Nursing: A Guide to Work in Early Years.* Oxford: Heinemann.

Taylor J. and Woods, M. (eds) (1998) *Early Childhood Studies*. London: Arnold.

9 The Reflective Practitioner

INTRODUCTION

The concept of reflective practice has become common in a wide range of different professional job roles, including social work, teaching and childcare. But what does it really mean and how do early years workers become reflective practitioners? This chapter explores the meaning and purpose of reflective practice in early years work. The role of reflective practice in improving and maintaining quality standards and a dynamic approach to change will be central themes. The contribution of individual practitioners to developing good practice will be discussed, as will the skills needed to become a reflective practitioner and the role of a reflective practitioner.

Defining Reflective Practice

Reflection, in this context, is the process by which early years workers ask the questions and seek the answers necessary to improve and maintain high standards in care and education. These questions can be about policy, your own work practices, institutional work practices, the link between theory and practice or the best ways of setting and achieving goals for change. In the simplest form, reflective practice is asking the questions, 'Am I doing a good job? 'How can I do a better job?'

Woods (1998) describes reflective practice as 'the hallmark of a genuine professional'. She mentions several aspects of reflective practice:

- theoretical understanding of childhood and child development
- the ability to interlink theory and observations
- drawing 'valid and reasoned interpretations and assessments' from observations
- using these assessments to inform planning and practice with children.

Woods goes on to state:

It is this which will enable us to make more appropriate or relevant provision or to enrich or amend the experiences we offer in order to foster each child's all-round development, learning, health and well-being.

(Woods, 1998: 27)

Put simply, reflective practice is about reviewing or analysing the work we do with children in terms of how best to contribute to their development, and using our experience and knowledge of theory to underpin this process. It is important that the process does not stop there. Having achieved a better understanding of the value of the experience we are offering children from this reflective process, it is vitally important to use this understanding to inform planning for change. Reflective practice is a dynamic process by which improvements in early years practice are continually being sought and achieved.

(Think) *A Chance to Think*

In many job roles we do much of our work automatically, without much thought as to why we do the things we do. For example, preparing activities for children in a care and education setting or organizing a trip to the local playground are activities that some of you may do on a regular basis. It is not possible to deeply analyse the motivations and outcomes for every single part of the job role. However, it is important to reflect on work practices and roles at times in order to ensure they are relevant and appropriate in terms of achieving high standards of care and education. The skills of a reflective practitioner are not necessarily difficult to develop. Learning the habit of using those skills may take more time.

Exercise 1

Think of an aspect of your role or the work in placement or your work setting. For example, a work practice or routine, the way in which the setting is laid out, the resources and how they are used, the priorities of staff and management.

Having chosen an aspect, consider it in terms of the following questions:

1 How far does it contribute to good standards of care and education?
2 To what extent are the needs of the children best met in this way?
3 How could it be done differently?
4 How could changes in this aspect enhance the children's experience?
5 To what extent is it in line with current thinking on best practice in this area?
6 How could I contribute in a more skilful way to this area of practice?

Discuss your reflections with a colleague or supervisor and ask for their views.

Theory and Practice

Reflective practice has developed in the caring professions in response to the need for higher levels of professionalism and increased flexibility and adaptability in service provision. The way in which we care for and educate children at the start of the twenty-first century is vastly different from practices of a hundred, fifty or even thirty years ago. But how does change come about? How did we move from the adult-centred practices of the Victorian age to the child-centred practices of the early twenty-first century?

Change comes in response to new ideas and theories about how best to care for and educate children. These new ideas and theories come from research, observations and analysis of data carried out by people working with children all over the world. They are based on ideas for improving practice which come from practitioners themselves. Theories are drawn from many different disciplines, including sociology, psychology, psychotherapy and biology. Research focuses on gathering and analysing data about the impact of different approaches to early years care and education on child health, welfare and development.

Often theory is built up over a period of time as new ideas are considered, tried and tested, modified and tested again. Changes often have to take place at policy level (legislation, social and organizational policy) before they take place at practice level. However, in some cases, changes taking place at practice level influence the development of new policy or legislation.

One example that may be familiar is the change in policy in the 1960s and 1970s from raising some young children in institutional care, to placing such children in substitute families. Although residential nurseries existed for very young children right up to the early 1970s, this form of care was dwindling a long time before then. But, why?

Research by John Bowlby from the 1950s showed the emotional and psychological damage inflicted on young children by institutional care in their early years. Studies of children in orphanages during and after the Second World War resulted in Bowlby (1953) developing his theory of attachment, which has continued to exercise a strong influence on early years childcare practice ever since. Robertson's study of children in hospital in the 1950s and the impact of separation from parents provided fresh evidence of the child's need for consistent care and the possible outcomes of separation (Robertson, 1953).

Other researchers developed Bowlby's attachment theory, emphasizing the need for young children to have a small, consistent and committed number of carers in their early years, in order to ensure healthy emotional and psychological development (Schaffer and Emerson, 1964).

Ainsworth's studies of children and separation identified different types of attachment (Ainsworth and Wittig, 1969; Ainsworth *et al.*, 1978). The impact of these theoretical developments on policy was not immediate or across the board. But practices and policies gradually changed and children are no longer separated from parents in hospital and, as a rule, young children in the UK are no longer cared for in institutions.

By the early 1980s, the vast majority of local authority social services departments had adopted the policy of placing children in their care who were under 12 years of age in foster homes where they could experience the continuation of family life and the committed support of a small number of carers.

This example shows us the complex relationship that exists between theory and practice and how theories are drawn from the observation and analysis of practice, but practice is meanwhile influenced by theory.

The role of individual practitioners is significant in terms of recognizing areas for change and developing new ways of working with children by applying theory to practice, or developing new theory through observation of practice. However change comes about, it is the result of reflections on existing practices and critical analysis of whether these particular practices are best meeting the needs of children.

The Individual Practitioner

Every individual practitioner potentially has a role to play in the process of developing theory and changing practice in early years care and education. Studies of children are usually done by practitioners, theories are often developed by practitioners and policy-makers usually start out as practitioners. This does not mean that all early years workers should be seeking to become academics, managers and nationally-renowned experts, although some will. However, the majority of early years workers have an important developmental role to play in their own workplace or organization.

In order to be part of the process of improving standards in childcare and education, individual practitioners need to build on their self-development skills and become reflective practitioners. This means developing the ability to analyse work practices and to reflect on areas for improvement. Through this process, you will be able to better understand the early years worker's role and the relevance of policies and practices in the work setting to good quality education and childcare. The reflective practitioner role could include some or even all of the following:

- keeping up-to-date with new developments, theories and ideas about early years education and care in general and/or particular specialisms or areas of interest
- developing analytical skills and a critical approach
- discussing ideas and theories with colleagues
- contributing to debates on issues through journals, conferences, staff development events and on courses of study
- observing children and analysing data gathered through observation
- continuing personal professional development
- introducing new educational and care practices into the workplace in agreement with colleagues
- supporting others to accept and welcome change.

These points will now be explored in more detail.

Keeping Up-to-Date with New Developments

Early years practitioners are generally qualified and trained at some stage of their career, usually earlier on when they are just starting out. During the process of early years education and training, information and ideas are assimilated and the early years worker starts to develop a view about how to be a good practitioner and to work well and safely in the educare of children. The student starts to understand the major theories of childhood and child development and to link these with practice experience on placement or in a work role. Successfully qualified and fully trained for the job role she has chosen, the practitioner takes up employment and starts to put knowledge and understanding into practice. The problem is, what happens next?

Early years care and education practices change over time in response to new theories or ideas about caring for and educating children, social and economic change and new legislation or policy. It is important that early years workers change also, to keep up-to-date with current thinking, policies and practices in early years education and childcare. As expectations of the job role change, the worker who has not kept up-to-date may become isolated and bewildered about what is required.

Keeping up with new developments in educare has a number of advantages, including the following:

- stimulating and maintaining analytical skills
- being aware of legislative and policy changes which impact on your work role
- exploring new job roles and opportunities for personal or career development
- understanding proposed changes to work practices
- maintaining an holistic view of the role of an early years worker
- further developing areas of special interest.

Keeping up with new developments can be time consuming and it is easy to argue that individual early years workers simply do not have the time and energy to do this. However, the consequences of not keeping up-to-date probably outweigh this argument in the majority of cases. Reading early years journals and magazines, books, newspapers or other publications, literature from relevant agencies or organizations, watching documentaries and accessing information from the Internet are all ways of gathering information about new developments in childcare and education. Discussing practices within the workplace, with colleagues or through other forums where early years workers meet is crucial to keeping up-to-date. Home carers such as childminders may have a particular need to involve themselves in group meetings in order to stay in touch with new ideas and developments. Professional organizations such as the National Childminding Association, the National Day Nursery Association, the Daycare Trust and British Association of Adoption and Fostering all have useful websites (see References).

Some of the most useful sources of up-to-date information are Government websites such as www.doh.gov.uk, www.ofsted.gov.uk, www.dfes.gov.uk and www.surestart.org.uk, which contain information about current developments and major documents affecting early years services. Other useful sources are newspaper archives on the net, such as www.guardianunlimited.co.uk.

Exercise 2

Make a list of the sources of information about developments in early years and care and education, relevant to your work or in general, which you use at the moment. Add other sources which you do not use at the moment, but which you are aware of. Share your list with colleagues, your supervisor, tutor and/or other students and add any other ideas to it. Decide how you could expand your use of sources of information by prioritizing what you may need or wish to know and deciding which sources of information are most accessible.

It is not enough just to read about new developments in education and care. Developing the ability to analyse critically information that is read, seen or heard is crucial to the process of becoming a reflective practitioner.

Developing Analytical Skills and a Critical Approach

There is no shortcut or easy way to develop skills in analysing and appraising the quality and content of new information. However, it is important to remember that not all ideas have the same value or level of credibility. The ability to critically analyse information depends on being able to decide how important or creditable information is, whether it is based on sound research or is an untested assertion and whether it makes sense in terms of your own understanding and experience of early years practice. When we first read theories of care and education or child development we try to make sense of them in terms of what we know about children. We ask ourselves questions about the link between the theory and what we know and we may observe children to test our understanding in more depth. Gradually, if the theory starts to make sense in terms of practice issues, and as we absorb new ideas and ways of understanding an aspect of early childhood, our practice may change in response.

In order to develop analytical skills, try the following:

- Read a range of different information about early years care and education, from different sources.
- Think about what you have read and discuss it with others.
- Compare theories and ideas about care and education with what you know from your own experience.
- Keep an open mind, but try not to accept everything at face value.
- Consider the reasons why certain care and education practices are common in most settings.

The last point is particularly relevant because it relates to an important aspect of reflective practice – the ability and willingness to question what is taken for granted.

Exercise 3

Go back to Exercise 1 and look at your answers to the questions. Did you find any aspect of practice in your work setting or placement which would have benefited from change? Write down your proposals for change in one area of practice and then write down the reasons why change might be resisted. This might include lack of resources, resistance to change on the part of staff, lack of familiarity with new ideas and systems, or reluctance to give up a well-known routine. What would be the benefits of change to the children, the staff and the parents? Write up your arguments and share them with a colleague or supervisor.

Discussing Ideas and Theories with Colleagues

Discussion gives us the chance to explore and refine ideas, to question others' views and opinions and to consider the gaps in our knowledge and understanding. For example, there is a debate in early years in the UK about whether children as young as 4 should be in school environments, when in many other European countries (and Australia and the USA) children do not start school until 6 or 7. There are different sides to the debate. Are we giving our youngest children a flying start with learning and skill development by early entry to school? Or are we denying them continuing play and exploration possibilities by introducing them to a formal curriculum at 3 and school at 4? Are these young children emotionally mature enough to be in school? Can they manage the self-care aspects of school as opposed to nursery?

Many such debates exist within the field of early years care and education. In order to make sense of them, it is important to read and to discuss the different views and arguments. Finding a colleague or supervisor to discuss different aspects of care and education with is a positive step towards becoming a reflective practitioner.

Contributing to Debates on Issues

Every early years worker has something to contribute to current debates about good practice in early years settings, but joining the debate may seem a daunting prospect. Working alone or in an institutional setting, you may feel you are simply not in a position to contribute your own views to the wider discussions taking place. However, if no one became involved in discussing good practice in early years care and education, there would be no possibility for change. There are a number of ways you can get involved:

- Read the trade magazines and write in to contribute to subject areas where you have knowledge, interest or particular expertise.
- Go to conferences, meetings on specific issues and local forums for discussion of early years issues.
- Attend short courses and day training events where possible.
- Access staff development where possible.
- Join a relevant association or professional body.

For example, many childminders are becoming increasingly involved in self-development activities, including local meetings, training and qualification courses and discussions about various aspects of childminding. The National Childminding Association supports childminders, providing information and advice through their membership scheme and keeping childminders in touch with relevant developments in childminding through publication of a quarterly magazine *Who Minds?* (www.ncma.org.uk).

Observing Children and Analysing Data

Most of what we know about the development of young children comes through observation and analysis of their behaviour, activities and play, and their interactions with each other and with adults. Observing children provides early years workers with a rich source of information about their needs and how best to meet them. Good practice in early years care and education is constantly reflected in the response of the children to the type of education and care they are receiving. Theories are developed through observation of children and the value of applying particular approaches to practice is supported by observational evidence.

Woods (1998) argues that the interlinking of theory and observation, based on a good understanding of childhood and child development and wide experience of working with children, is at the heart of 'sensitive educare'.

For example, if we want to know whether an activity designed to promote an understanding of the properties of different liquids has enhanced the children's knowledge and experience, then we would observe their involvement in the activity and possibly their play at a later stage. This would give us information about what the children have learned, whether they have absorbed that learning into existing schema, and how that learning may have altered and extended the children's perceptions. The value of such knowledge is enormous. It provides the basis for improving the quality of the children's learning experiences, for building on what the children already know and for extending the learning into new and challenging areas. Without this knowledge, early years workers may carry on providing children with the similar types of activities again and again without any real understanding of whether the children are gaining from the experience.

Reflective practice is dependent on observational assessment of children and their activities to produce the sort of evaluation that extends and improves the individual and workplace standards of educare for the children.

Observations are an essential part of most early years courses, but although many early years workers continue observing on a regular basis once they have completed their course of study, in some job roles this is less consistent. There is some evidence that staff in schools have difficulty finding time to observe (Bennett *et al.,* 1997) Even students have difficulty carrying out observations at times, because of the busy nature of many early years settings. Yet few early years workers would dispute the value of observation for assessing individual development, evaluating the outcomes of an activity in terms of the children's learning and development, or targeting a particular area of concern.

Observation is crucial to the dynamic process of reflective practice, because it provides the data to analyse and to compare with theoretical knowledge, in order to reach conclusions that can inform planning for change.

Exercise 4

Complete an observation within your placement or work setting or refer to an observation you have already completed. Write down how the data gathered through observation was used as part of the process of reflective practice, and how analysis of the information was or could be used to enhance the quality of educare in the work or placement setting. Share your notes with a colleague or supervisor.

Continuing Personal Professional Development

Professional development is the process by which individual workers can maintain, update and extend their skills for work. This could involve higher level professional training, specialist training or developing totally new skill areas. Early years workers are professionals in a dynamic field of work. The context and content of early years work are changing and developing through time and it is vital that practitioners change in response. In addition, the technological revolution has made acquiring and updating a range of information technology and communications (ITC) skills necessary in virtually every job role. Keeping in touch with new developments can seem daunting to the most enthusiastic 'lifelong learner', but gaining the habit of learning can also be exciting and enjoyable.

Initial training provides the basic skills, knowledge and theoretical background for many early years work roles. Maintaining existing skills and developing new ones can be achieved in a number of ways:

- staff development, including short courses and day events, possibly offered by professional organizations or training agencies
- higher level qualifications including advanced diplomas, degree level courses, Foundation Degrees
- specialist training focusing on particular areas of work, for example working with children with special needs
- IT, Internet and other ITC courses

- distance learning, Open University and other courses requiring minimum attendance at an institution
- personal development through individual study, possibly in response to new requirements of the job role.

Exercise 5

Try to draw up a personal development plan by considering the following questions:

1 What further learning would help me to work effectively in my chosen job role?
2 Which of my skills need updating or developing further?
3 Am I up-to-date with information and communication technologies?
4 Which specialist areas of working with young children do I want or need to know more about?

Then consider the following questions:

1 What sort of training or staff development is available to me now?
2 What might be provided in the future?
3 Are there other sources of training and education locally and if so what is available?
4 Have I been for careers advice recently and found out what is on offer?
5 Are there any professional organizations or bodies related to my work role which provide training or education?

The answers to these questions will be very different depending on whether you are a full-time student or you are currently in work. However, finding out about and making use of the resources around you is something that may be useful to any early years worker at whatever stage of their working life. Discuss the outcomes of your investigations with a colleague, supervisor or tutor.

A belief in the value of learning new skills and gaining new knowledge is central to the concept of reflective practice. Reflective practitioners are able to review their own work and by doing so, become aware of areas for self-development. This does not mean that all early years workers must be constantly involved in formal education and training. It does mean that if there are aspects of your work which you need to know more about in order to work to a high standard, then you are willing to take steps to fill the gaps, whether by reading a book or going on a course or discussing the issue with an expert colleague.

Introducing New Care and Education Practices into the Workplace

Change is a central theme in how we approach the education and care of young children. This does not mean that we need to alter the routines and habits of care and education that we are involved in on a daily or weekly basis! But early years workers need to be aware of the need for reviewing and developing childcare and education practices in line with new ideas, policies and theories. Reflective practitioners consider not only their own contribution to the quality of the care and education they are involved in, but also whether that care and education best meets the needs of the children. Sometimes routines and practices almost gain a life of their own. They become such ingrained habits that we cease to question their validity, or ask the question, 'Why do we do the things we do, in the way we do them?' Some routines and practices arise because of particular sets of circumstances, budget limitations or current beliefs about best practice. These factors may all be valid at the time, but have little relevance five years later. It is important to regularly review work practices in order to ensure they remain current and valid, and meet equal opportunities objectives and the needs of the children.

Exercise 6

Look at Exercise 1 in this chapter again and consider whether there is anything you could add to your answer. Draw up a plan for introducing change in respect of your chosen area of practice and decide how you would introduce your ideas to your colleagues or supervisor.

Supporting Others to Accept and Welcome Change

Change can be challenging for some and downright terrifying for others. Not all colleagues will accept change easily and some may be resistant. Individuals become used to certain ideas and concepts and ways of working, and may not be easily persuaded to reconsider the current relevance of these. Supporting colleagues through change involves tact and diplomacy, the ability to present arguments and plans simply and coherently and the ability to empathize with others' concerns and help them to overcome these.

But why do some resist change? Possible reasons include:

- fear of the unknown
- fear that they may not be able to do the job properly if it changes
- lack of understanding of the reasons for change
- lack of support
- the comfortable nature of well-established patterns and routines in work.

THE REFLECTIVE PRACTITIONER

Reflective practitioners need to be able to carry others with their ideas and approaches in order to achieve better standards.

Exercise 7

Read the case study below and decide how the worker could introduce her plans for change effectively, overcome any resistance to her ideas and support colleagues to make changes in their work practices.

MEG

Meg, a nursery worker, felt that there was a tokenistic approach to supporting and celebrating cultural diversity in the nursery that did not truly reflect the value of different cultures. Meg felt that different approaches were needed to help British Asian children in particular feel that their cultural norms and values were understood and appreciated. She drew up a plan which involved staff gaining more knowledge and information about everyday cultural practices among the local British Asian community by talking to parents and children and involving them in choosing books, display material and activities to reflect their culture more appropriately.

Getting Support to Become a Reflective Practitioner

In order to achieve better standards in their own work and influence change in a wider context, early years workers need to get support for themselves. Discussion with experienced others is invaluable in terms of forming ideas about good practice and how to achieve high standards by developing these ideas within the job role. Discussion with a colleague, supervisor, tutor or friend who acts as a mentor can help the process of linking theory and practice, analyse the value of new ideas and concepts and develop a problem-solving approach to areas of work which require change. A mentor or supporter does not have to be involved with you on a formal basis, but there are a number of basic requirements of the role:

- expertise and experience in the work role
- ability to think objectively and analytically
- confidentiality
- open to new ideas and concepts and able to discuss these
- involved in own self-development
- committed to raising standards and achieving good practice
- accessible.

Possibly the best situation is if you have a colleague with whom you can share ideas on a mutual basis, providing each other with mentoring support.

Supervisors can sometimes offer managerial support for your self-development activities and provide access to staff development. Supervisors can also help to implement agreed changes to work practices. In some job roles, there are appraisal systems, which, properly used, focus on individual staff targets and staff development needs in order to meet those targets.

Other support can be gained from tutors, professional bodies or forums, other agency professionals and parents.

Conclusions

Becoming a reflective practitioner is a gradual process of learning different skills and absorbing new ways of approaching early years work. It can feel like an uphill struggle at times, especially if there is resistance to change around you or lack of resources to achieve your goals. However, being a reflective practitioner can be highly rewarding, as through reflection, analysis, comparison of theory and practice and review of outcomes you learn more about the process of achieving good standards in early years care and education. Reflective practice is stimulating and demanding, and an essential component of good practice.

REFERENCES AND FURTHER READING

Ainsworth, M. D. S. and Wittig, B. A. (1969) 'Attachment and exploratory behaviour of one year olds in strange situations', in B. M. Foss, (ed.) *Determinants of Infant Behaviour*. London: Methuen.

Ainsworth, M. D. S., Blehdr, M., Aters, E. and Wall, S. (1978) *Patterns of Attachment*. Hillsdale, NJ: Lawrence Erlbaum.

Bennett, N., Wood, L. and Rogers, S. (1997) *Teaching Through Play – Teacher's Thinking and Classroom Practice*. Buckingham: OU Press.

Bowlby, J. (1953) *Child Care and the Growth of Love*. London: Pelican.

British Association of Adoption and Fostering www.baaf.org.uk

Bruce, T. (1991) *Time to Play in Early Childhood Education*. London: Hodder and Stoughton.

Daycare Trust www.daycare.org.uk

Hobart, C. and Frankel, J. (1999) *Childminding: A Guide to Good Practice*. Cheltenham: Stanley Thornes.

National Childminding Association www.ncma.org.uk

National Day Nurseries Association www.ndna.org.uk

Robertson, J. (1953) *A Two Year Old Goes to Hospital* (film)

Robertson, J. (1953) *Going to Hospital with Mother* (film) www.robertsonfilms.info

Schaffer, H. and Emerson, P. (1964) 'The development of social attachments in infancy', *Child Development*, **29**: 94.

Woods, M. (1998) 'Early Childhood Studies – first principles', in J. Taylor and M. Woods (eds) *Early Childhood Studies: An Holistic Introduction*. London: Arnold.

10 Conclusions

Good practice in early years care and education is not a single issue or skill. It relates to a wide range of philosophical issues and ways of working with young children. As early years workers, your knowledge, skills and abilities and your understanding of current issues in early years care and education are all crucial to the process of developing good practice. Understanding theory and being able to apply it in practice situations is another important theme. Perhaps the single most important contribution to achieving good practice is the attitude of practitioners within early years. Willingness to question practice, to apply knowledge and to further develop skills is part of the process of becoming a reflective practitioner as outlined in Chapter 9.

Early years care and education has never been static. Changes in philosophy, methods of care and education and structures of service delivery are all part of the history of childcare and education. At the start of the twenty-first century, debates about quality in early years care and education continue to occupy practitioners and theorists. The introduction of Early Learning Goals for pre-school children and the increasingly structured nature of the pre-school curriculum continue to be critically analysed. International perspectives offer us alternative models of early years care and education. In many other countries, young children start school at 6 or later and the pre-school curriculum is less focused on formal learning. The roles of structed and child-directed play in early childhood learning and development is contested, with sharp divisions between both theorists and practitioners.

One of the questions that may have arisen as you read this book is, 'How do we know if good practice is being achieved?' Assessing good practice is closely linked with assessing quality in early years care and education. The most obvious measure of good practice in any early years setting is your latest OFSTED report. However,

OFSTED standards should be seen as minimum rather than maximum, and relying on a single measure of quality can make us complacent about achievements and standards. No single measure can cover all aspects of quality. Measuring quality should not be confined to single events, widely spaced in time, but should be an ongoing cycle.

The method of assessment of quality in early years care and education depends on which aspects are being assessed, according to Katz (1992) who suggests two main models:

1 The top-down approach, focusing on structural issues such as staff-child ratios, and the standards of staff, resources and the environment.
2 The bottom-up perspective, which focuses on the experience of the child in the environment as a basis for assessing quality.

(from Heaslip, 1994)

Heaslip (1994) goes on to argue that in order to assess the 'basics' of 'educare' – the 'absolute educational priorities' – then the bottom-up model needs to be used for some areas of assessment. He defines the 'basics' as:

- a child's belief in herself and a positive self-image
- a respect for the individuality of others.

We could argue that good practice in early years care and education is aimed at helping each child achieve these 'basics'. Heaslip uses the bottom-up model to analyse play, but it could be extended to analyse all aspects of the child's experience in educare settings.

A bottom-up assessment may involve asking some of the following questions to try and determine whether the 'basics' are being achieved for each child:

- Does the child have genuine choices in the setting over the toys she uses and the activities and play she is involved in?
- Can the child make mistakes and learn from them without any sense of failure?
- Are rules sensible, democratic and at a minimum?
- Is a sense of 'ownership' of the setting fostered so that the child feels not only that he belongs, but that he is a central member of the group?
- Is the child's unique sense of self acknowledged, fostered and respected within her own wider culture and personal characteristics?
- Is adult involvement with children sensitive, based on observation and appropriate to the child's needs?
- Are adults able to allow the children to have control in terms of activities, rules and decision-making about some aspects of the setting?
- Is genuine praise given?
- Are parents viewed as partners and experts on their own children?

These are not all the questions we might ask if we were trying to assess educare provision from the bottom-up. There are many more. These questions are, however, a starting point for considering how we can focus on the 'basics'.

A Chance to Think

Assessing quality in a workplace or placement we are familiar with can be difficult. It may be hard to achieve an objective view. Looking at the experience from the child's point of view can bring some important issues into focus and give a new perspective on familiar routines and structures.

Exercise 1

Read the questions above and try to answer them in respect of one or more children in your workplace or placement. Share your answers with a colleague or supervisor. Does a bottom-up assessment give you different feedback on some aspects of the educare offered? What other questions might it be useful to ask?

Perhaps the most important issue here is to ensure that each child feels involved and valued. A sense of being important and respected is crucial to children's growing sense of identity, and their ability to value and respect others. Achieving this 'basic' lays the foundations for learning and development in the child's future. Early years workers who know they have achieved this with the children they care for and educate can claim to be working to high standards. As one boy of 5 said, when passing the nursery he had left for reception class six months earlier: 'I wonder how on earth they are managing without me?' He clearly carried a strong sense of his own value from his experiences at the nursery.

You have probably realized that looking at good practice issues under separate headings is an artificial divide. Good practice issues may have different aspects, but the values on which they are based are fundamentally the same. Early years workers develop these values through their studies and through relating work experiences to both theory and current concepts and ideas about quality childcare and education. It is important to build up our own sense of good practice, which becomes an automatic, internalized part of the work we do. Guidelines and codes of practice, statements of principles and legal and policy statements are all useful to remind us of the areas in which good practice is most important. But good practice should not be confined to these areas. It should permeate all early years work and be part of all planning, delivering, monitoring and review processes to do with an educare service for children. Building knowledge and skills in this area may be hard work at first, but gaining confidence and an enhanced sense of purpose about the work you do is the reward. Remember that there are many, many other practitioners who are working to provide quality educare. Find your own support systems among them as you work towards becoming a reflective practitioner yourself. Good luck!

REFERENCES AND FURTHER READING

Heaslip, P. (1994) 'Making play work in the classroom', in Moyles (1994).

Katz, L. G. (1992) 'Multiple perspectives on the quality of early childhood programmes.' Unpublished paper given at the Second European Conference on the *Quality of Early Childhood Education*, August, Worcester College of Higher Education.

Moyles, J. R. (ed.) (1994) *The Excellence of Play*. Buckingham: OU Press.

Appendix:
Answers to Exercises

Chapter 1

Exercise 1

1 Sam has a right to care and education that will meet his needs as a child with learning disabilities. Amy has a right to physical safety.
2 Both children need support in this situation.
3 Discuss Sam's needs for additional support with his parents and other staff. Monitor him more closely and use 'time out' if he is getting agitated, making it clear this is not a punishment. Plan approaches to helping him control his impulses more in collaboration with his parents. Explore themes within the group of children about respect and care for each other, without focusing on Sam. Explain equal opportunities policy to Amy's father and acknowledge that his daughter's safety is an important issue. Be open with him about your plans to support both children more effectively.

Exercise 3

Hitting children with belts or other objects is no longer considered an acceptable form of punishment, mainly because of increased social awareness of child abuse.

Locking children in their rooms or cupboards would be considered cruel and emotionally abusive in current times.

Depriving children of food or drink as a punishment is no longer acceptable, because the parent would be failing to meet the child's basic needs.

Smacking on the hand with a ruler, which was a form of punishment sometimes used in schools in the past, is outlawed along with other methods of corporal punishment in state schools.

Exercise 4

1 It is important not to make any assumptions about children and their families. There is a wide range of family types in British society and many children live with one parent, step-parents, foster carers, grandparents or adoptive families.
2 The children could be asked to bring photos that they like of themselves and their families or have them taken in school.
3 Be sensitive to the many variations in family types, recognize that not all children have happy memories of the past and remember that not all families have cameras.
4 Ask for or take a photo of Sandra and her family now.

Exercise 5

1 The staff member's standard of care may be different for British Asian children if her prejudices influence her attitude and behaviour towards them.
2 No – by supporting the racist comment, the staff member implicitly encourages the parent to express such views. The attitude expressed within the conversation may be considered to be the philosophy within the nursery.
3 The reply may have included comments that you believe it is positive to have children from a range of cultures within the nursery and that the nursery supports equality for all children.
4 Discuss the issue again with the manager, emphasizing the discriminatory nature of the remarks and the possible impact on children of supporting racist attitudes. Suggest that staff development could be arranged for all staff to look at practical approaches to dealing with racism and to find ways of supporting the self-esteem of all children.

Chapter 2

Exercise 1

1 Acknowledge that Paula is tired and that she has suffered a disruption in familiar routines. School may be difficult for her and she may be finding all the changes hard to cope with. Meet Paula with a healthy snack after school, as she may be hungry, and arrange quiet activities in the afternoon, perhaps even a nap.
2 Ask the parents for their advice and whether they are concerned about Paula in any way.
3 Talk to school staff about Paula and check if they have concerns about her.

Exercise 2

1 Set clear boundaries around Nathan's disruptive behaviour, using 'time out' and giving him permission to go to a quiet corner if he cannot settle. Give Nathan support with his play and activities, but explain that other children need this time too. Find some small responsibilities for him to take on, such as helping put toys away or clear up. Help Nathan build concentration by finding him activities that interest him and by offering support.
2 Discuss possible approaches and agree a plan.
3 Discuss your plan with his mother and agree common strategies in nursery and at home. Ask his mother about the sort of activities which Nathan enjoys at home.

Exercise 3

Children could be asked to do a word storm about the activity or draw pictures to describe how they felt about it. You would need to prepare the children by explaining that it was OK to be honest and that you wanted to know if they had enjoyed the activity or not. The children could role-play being 'judges' or a TV panel making a decision. The children would need to know that they would not hurt your feelings if they made negative comments. The children could be asked to suggest ways of making the activity more interesting. You would need to listen carefully, without interrupting or interpreting the comments the children made. Their comments should be written down as they were said. It should be clear from your non-verbal language that you value the children's views and opinions. The feedback should be presented to others as it was presented to you, with no interpretation. The process by which the feedback was given should be explained.

Chapter 4

Exercise 5

Children should be given opportunity to talk to you quietly and in confidence at break times, during outdoor play and when you are helping the child with an activity. Staff need to be aware that a child may be looking for an opportunity to talk and to make that opportunity if necessary, for example by asking the child to help you with a task or to stay and help clear up for a few minutes. Give the child a chance to speak by being quiet and listening.

Chapter 5

Exercise 2

1 Jas needs opportunity to develop social skills in a secure environment through play and activities with adults and other children. She needs to develop confidence in new situations and people. Jas needs to feel that her cultural and religious background is important and valued in the setting. She needs support to learn through play and other activities as a deaf child and she may need extra help to communicate effectively in the nursery setting.
2 The nursery needs to be sensitive to Jas's lack of social experience and to recognize that she will need the support of a parent and a key worker to settle in. Jas may need adult help joining the group, learning social and play skills and integrating with the other children. The nursery staff need to ensure that Jas's cultural and religious background is reflected in images and activities in the nursery and that due consideration is given to any relevant cultural norms, e.g. food, hygiene, clothes. Assumptions should not be made about these issues in respect of Jas's individual needs. Jas may need to learn to communicate through signing and others should be able to sign to her, including the other children.
3 The nursery staff will need to know about any religious and cultural practices, e.g. diet, that Jas should follow during her time at nursery. They should also find out how profound Jas's hearing impairment is and any decisions the

family has made about how Jas will learn to communicate. If Jas is learning signs, the extent of her knowledge should be established. The language(s) in which Jas is learning to communicate need to be known. The support available for hearing impaired children should be explored along with any additional resources available to help Jas with her learning.

4 Help with establishing the extent of Jas's hearing impairment and the likely impact this may have on the development of her communication skills. Options available to Jas and her family in terms of language development and support available for children learning to communicate non-verbally. The role of specialist teachers for hearing impaired children may be central in this process. Help may be available from the LEA (assessment and learning support), social services and voluntary organizations as well as the health services.

Exercise 3

1 Eddie needs to develop a sense of security through stability and continuity in his environment and care givers. He needs social and language development opportunities, and to build confidence. He may need support to learn to play. Eddie needs to be encouraged to eat and enjoy a range of foods.
2 The nursery could meet Eddie's needs by supporting and helping him to access play and to join the group of children. Adult support and a phased entry may help in this. A key worker with whom Eddie could build a secure relationship may contribute to his feelings of safety and security. Eddie may need to be encouraged to try different foods and to be active in order to build an appetite. He may need help from a speech therapist.
3 Eddie may feel very insecure because of his recent loss of familiar carers. He may fear abandonment. Eddie may have difficulty joining the group and developing social and play skills, because of his insecurity and language delays. He may be frightened and upset. Eddie may find another new diet hard to cope with and may refuse to eat unfamiliar foods.

Chapter 6

Exercise 2

The potential hazards of outdoor activities include poisonous plants, sharp plants, chemicals such as slug pellets, dog faeces, broken glass or other rubbish. Water play involves risk of drowning, slipping on wet surfaces, and getting too cold. Equipment may be unstable and children could fall from it. Bikes and trikes could go out of control or the child could fall off.

Outside areas should be regularly checked for hazards, activities should be monitored and supervised and equipment properly assembled and checked for faults.

Exercise 8

During a child protection investigation, you should remain calm and objective. Continue to behave as normally as possible with the parents. Give the child attention and quiet times to talk and remain warm and affectionate towards him. Do not dwell on the investigation but answer the child's questions if you can. Make sure the child knows that he has your support.

This might be difficult if you reported the abuse. The child may be withdrawn from your care or the setting. If not, do not get into arguments with parents, who may be angry. Continue to be supportive to the child. Acknowledge that it is a difficult situation for you all.

Chapter 7

Exercise 1

1 Ian will have more consistent care and his needs will be better met. Positive relationships with the parents will promote good communication with them. Knowledge of the possible difficulties they are facing may improve your empathy with the parents and help you to offer appropriate support. Ian will settle well and benefit from the placement in terms of his learning and development.
2 Establishing open communication patterns and supportive relationship with the parents should encourage a co-operative approach to problem-solving if a difficulty arises.

Exercise 3

Howard's basic needs for food, warmth and supervision may not be being met. He may not be receiving enough stimulation and this may affect his cognitive and language development. He may be insecurely attached to his mother.

Sara may need more time and attention from her parents. Her emotional needs may be being neglected. She may be anxious and fearful because of the rows.

Donovan may be too isolated, lacking social contacts and outside support.

Carl may be missing out on attention, especially from his father. He may feel 'scapegoated' because he might feel he is responsible for his father's absences. He may be resentful of the new baby.

Jasmine may feel insecure and afraid. The racist comments may be emotionally damaging and affect her self-image and self-esteem. Her social development may be affected by the negative attitudes of others and social isolation.

Exercise 4

1 The mother may suffer additional stress, coping with all the children. Drew will miss out on regular routines and the stimulation of being in nursery.
2 Drew's mother might be experiencing problems with money, coping with the children, the house and the social services investigation. She may feel angry, upset, frightened, guilty and ashamed.
3 The nursery staff could try to maintain the relationship, offer support and advice, acknowledge feelings.
4 A home visit by a staff member could be used to explain that Drew and his mother were both welcome at nursery and that she was not being judged.

DAVEY

The parents may have chosen Minton Street because the environment seems to be child-centred with a clearly stated philosophy and purpose. The child-centered approach seems to be evident in the whole setting, including the head's office. The atmosphere of 'purposeful and enjoyable activity' implies that the children are learning and having fun. The general welcome from staff and the enthusiasm with which they share information implies an open and honest approach to partnership with parents and a staff team who are committed to their work. There is evidence of community links and support for parents. The environment is pleasant and attractive, reflecting the range of types of family using the nursery and a culture of inclusivity for all children and families.

A warm welcome may help to allay fears these parents may have about the nursery's approach to children with special needs. It may help these parents to feel that their child could belong in this nursery and that support would be there for the child and themselves. They may feel that this initial contact is the basis for a good partnership with the nursery.

Exercise 5

Sam may feel ridiculed and dismissed. He may have missed out on education himself and be anxious that this should not happen to his daughter. She may be aware of conflict and become less confident. Sam could be asked to spend time in the setting, to support his child through play and he could be given books explaining how children learn. He could be reassured that his child is making progress.

Anjie may feel criticized and judged. The child may be withdrawn from the setting or become aware of the tension between the adults and react to this. The problem in the morning could be discussed in non-critical terms and the worker could help to find a solution.

Yasmin's mother may feel isolated in a hostile environment. Yasmin may be missing social contact and stimulation. The group leader could spend time with Yasmin's mother, talking to her and finding out about her. She could introduce her to other parents.

Peter may be aware of the tension and feel anxious and upset. His mother may be upset because the staff member did not approach her directly. The worker and the mother could discuss the problem and look for solutions together.

Exercise 7

1 The children are not being properly supervised and there is too much responsibility being placed on Chantelle's 9-year-old brother.
2 Discuss your concerns with the mother. Pass them on to the social worker.
3 Sensitive, non-accusatory, supportive and tactful communication skills are needed.
4 Be a role model, explain the risks, give advice, and listen to the mother.

187

Chapter 8

✎ Exercise 3

1 Elly's class teacher and the headteacher need to know. Record the information.
2 Other staff may need to know that Mark may need extra support at present. Do not record the information.
3 No one should be told about Rose and Daisy's father. Do not record it.
4 All staff need to know about Frank and Dean's father and the situation should be recorded.

✎ Exercise 5

1 You may have concerns about possible physical abuse.
2 The designated child protection liaison teacher should be told.
3 No one else needs to know at this stage.

✎ Exercise 6

The doctor should be told in order to provide Cathy with medical support.

Other professionals should be taking precautions against infection as part of their job role. Others on the list are at very low levels of risk. The school may be informed if they are aware of the issues and will be supportive. Revealing Cathy's HIV status to others could lead to her being stigmatized and socially isolated.

Glossary

Anti-discriminatory practice – work practices which aim to reduce discrimination against groups and individuals and to promote equality of opportunity for all

Area Child Protection Procedures – guidelines to all agencies and individuals involved with children in terms of their role in identifying and taking steps to protect children from abuse and neglect

Bilingual – speaking and understanding more than one language

CACHE – Council for Awards in Children's Care and Education

Care Order – a court order under the Children Act, 1989, which transfers the care of the child from the parent(s) to the Local Authority

Care Proceedings – the legal process including the court hearing by which the Local Authority applies for a Care Order in respect of a child or children

Case conference – a meeting of professionals and possibly parents and other relevant non-professionals to make decisions or recommendations about the care and welfare of a child or children

Citizenship – the status and rights accorded to members of a society

Culture – the values and attitudes which are held by a particular social group and the behaviours and customs which are considered normal within that group

Disability – any impairment which has a significant or long-term negative impact on an individual's ability to perform the normal everyday activities of living

Discrimination – treating individuals or groups of people differently (usually less fairly) on the basis of negative views of that individual or group

Educare – a term describing both the concept of education and care as inextricable from each other, and the practices and settings in which children are both educated and cared for

Emergency Protection Order – a court order under the Children Act 1989, by which children

considered to be at risk of 'significant harm' can be removed from their parent(s) on an emergency basis

Equal Opportunities – treating all equally in terms of recognizing and meeting individual needs

Ethnic – relating to different cultural groups, in that ethnic minorities are cultural groups which are in a minority within the wider society

'Free-flow play' – play which is child-directed and where the adult role is supportive, not directive

Gender – the different cultural and social expectations of males and females, which are socially created and absorbed by children as part of their socialization process

HIV – Human Immuno-deficiency Virus

Holistic – in this context, relating to the whole child as opposed to one aspect of the child's development, learning, behaviour or ability

Interagency – involving more than one agency such as health, education, social services

IT – information technology

ICT – information and communications technology

Legal framework – the set of laws and regulations which govern practices within a particular field

'Looked after children' – children in the care of the local authority

Multicultural – relating to more than one cultural group

Multi-disciplinary – relating to more than one professional group

NVQ – National Vocational Qualification

Prejudice – the prejudgement or assumptions and biases about individuals or groups based on stereotypes of that individual or group

Racism – prejudice based on perceptions of an individual's or group's racial origins

SVQ – Scottish Vocational Qualification

Stereotype – a firmly held and rigid view of an individual or group, which incorporates assumptions about that person's or group's characteristics and behaviour

Index